KU-779-882

Welcome to Porto

Opening up dramatically from the banks of the Rio Douro, Porto enthrals with its historic centre, sumptuous food and wine, high-spirited nightlife and charismatic locals. Walk in its higgledy-piggledy medieval lanes, get briefed on the nuances of port in hillside lodges, take a tram to the sea in Foz and you'll fall madly in love with this most soulful of cities.

LONDON BOROUGH OF WANDSWORTH	
9030 00006 6357 2	
Askews & Holts	14-Feb-2019
914.691504	£7.99
	WW18015952

Ponte de Dom Luís I (p44)
MARICS / SHUTTERSTOCK ©

Top Sights

Sé

Porto's crowning glory cathedral. **p34**

VADIM PETRAKOV / SHUTTERSTOCK ©

Igreja de São Francisco

Beauty in the baroque. **p36**

Palácio da Bolsa

Porto's resplendent stock exchange palace. **p38**

Museu Nacional Soares dos Reis

Colossal fine arts collection. **p80**

Centro Português de Fotografia

Arresting photography in a former jail. **p82**

JEFF GREENBERG / AGE FOTOSTOCK ©

Jardins do Palácio de Cristal

Porto's most romantic hilltop gardens. **p112**

FOTOKON / SHUTTERSTOCK ©

Serralves

Cutting-edge art, avant-garde architecture. **p136**

Casa da Música

Architectural heavyweight with world-class acoustics. **p124**

Eating

Porto's food scene has gone through the roof in recent years. Hot trends include petiscos (small Portuguese plates, ideal for sharing), lazy weekend brunches, creative vegetarian buffet-style restaurants, urban-cool restaurants putting imaginative riffs on global flavours, and old-school taverns championing slow food. And don't forget the temptation of cafes, delis and patisseries around nearly every corner.

Soul Food

Porto is sprinkled with family-run *tascas* and *tabernas*, no-frills, cheap-as-chips places filled with cheek-by-jowl tables and local chatter. At some, you'll still get change from a €10 note at lunchtime. Here classics have never gone out of fashion – the *francesinha* (a gut-buster of roast meat, cheese-and-egg-topped sandwich) or *tripas à moda do Porto* (hearty offal and white bean stew), for instance.

Gourmet Heaven

Forward-thinking, fearlessly experimental chefs have put Porto firmly on the gastro map, with surprise tasting menus prepared with flawless execution, experimental finesse and a nod to the seasons. Names like Pedro Lemos and Ricardo Costa (the Yeatman) have put the city on the Michelin map, while Rui Paula pairs showstopping architecture with menus extolling the virtues of Portuguese produce.

Portuguese

Flor dos Congregados (p63) Rustic, welcoming family-run number, playing up seasonal Portuguese cuisine.

Cantinho do Avillez (p49) Portuguese star chef José Avillez puts riffs on Portuguese flavours at this modish bistro.

Tripeiro (p64) Modern-rustic restaurant doling out no-nonsense Portuguese classics, including Porto-style tripe and bean stew.

Casa Agrícola (p131) Sidling up to a chapel, this smart Boavista fave serves the like of *cataplanas* (seafood stews).

O Caraças (p91) A mother and her daughters run this sweet tavern like a tight ship, serving up Portuguese soul food.

Tapas & Tascas

Taberna do Largo (p46) Tasting platters, hand-picked wines and a relaxed ambience.

DZMITRY RYSHCHUK / SHUTTERSTOCK ©

Cantina 32 (p48) Imaginative, insanely tasty *petiscos* in an industro-cool setting. Terrace for warm-weather dining.

Tapabento (p63) Cosy bistro for sharing plates and carefully chosen wines.

Porta 4 (p90) Super-friendly, blink-and-you'll-miss-it tapas place in Miragaia.

Tascö (p64) We love the sleek Scandi look and *petiscos* at this central haunt.

Fine Dining

Vinum (p105) Hilltop gourmet restaurant, with an excellent cellar to boot.

Pedro Lemos (p140) The chef takes pride in local, seasonal sourcing at this two-Michelin-starred stunner.

Antiqvvm (p120) Romance, captivating views and one Michelin star.

Yeatman (p104) Chef Ricardo Costa pulls off a class act at this two-Michelin-starred restaurant.

Euskalduna Studio (p65) Tables are like gold dust at this intimate, experimental choice. Book ahead.

MUU (p65) Urban-cool steakhouse with choice cuts of meat.

World Flavours & Fusion

Belos Aires (p92) A little drop of Argentina in Miragaia, with terrific steaks, Malbec and *empanadas*.

Frida (p92) Boho-flavoured Mexican, with cuisine that packs a punch.

Mistu (p92) Porto's neo-Moorish sophisticate, with nods to Asia and South America.

Flow (p64) Go with it for clean, bright Mediterranean flavours in a pretty inner courtyard.

Eat Like a Local

○ The *couvert* (bread, olives, pâté etc) brought to the table as an appetiser costs. Pay for what you eat or feel free to send it away.

Drinking & Nightlife

While Porto isn't going to steal the clubbing crown any time soon, tripeiros (Porto residents) love to get their groove on, especially in the Galerias, with its speakeasy-style bars and the party spilling out onto the streets. With just enough urban edge to keep the scene fresh-faced, a night out here can easily jump from indie clubs to refined rooftop bars.

Districts

Porto's nightlife scene is incredibly chilled, swinging with ease from beachfront haunts in Foz to river-view bars in Vila Nova de Gaia. The backstreets of Ribeira brim with wine bars. As the night wears on, Galerias is party central, with bar-rammed streets where you can drift from one bar to the next as the mood and music takes you.

That's Entertainment

Porto has never been one to shy away from a party, and its entertainment scene is upbeat and eclectic. Besides performing arts and classical music, there are live-music haunts homing in on home-grown talent, jazz and fado bars, cultural venues and artsy enclaves. For the top places you'll need to reserve tickets, but smaller venues often stage gigs for free.

Bars

Prova (p51) Diogo shares his love of Portuguese wine at this stylish number.

Wine Quay Bar (p51) Sunset is prime-time viewing at this riverside wine bar.

Era uma Vez em Paris (p66) Bordello-chic bar evoking Paris in the 1920s.

Aduela (p66) Retro-cool haunt with vintage furnishings.

Museu d'Avó (p66) Glorious time-warp of a bar.

Café Candelabro (p69) Artsy cafe-bookshop, spilling out onto a pavement terrace.

Cocktails & Beer

Wall (p69) Urban-cool, backlit, insanely popular Galerias bar for a mojito.

Letraria (p66) Craft beers, a chilled vibe and a tree-shaded garden.

Pinguim Café (p93) For quality gin cocktails and a boho vibe, this is the perfect tonic.

Armazém da Cerveja (p72) Some 70 brews on offer and a beer garden.

EMILY MCAULIFFE / LONELY PLANET ©

Catraio (p94) A shop-cum-bar placing the accent on Portuguese craft beers.

Performing Arts

Casa da Música (p133) Porto's cultural behemoth, with concerts from classical to jazz.

Teatro Nacional São João (p71) Porto's foremost theatre wows with dance, drama and live music.

Coliseu do Porto (p71) Art deco theatre staging gigs, dance productions and plays.

Gardens & Terraces

Miradouro Ignez (p120) Sundown drinks, snacks and river gazing.

Praia da Luz (p140) Tucked-away beach bar for sundowners in Foz.

Mirajazz (p93) Steps lead to this terrace, with a cool crowd and jazz beats.

Intrigo (p92) Peer out across the rooftops to the river at this hidden terrace.

360° Terrace Lounge (p106) Arresting views of Porto's historic centre.

Live Music

Breyner 85 (p94) Live music from rock to jazz and blues, plus Sunday-night jam sessions.

Plano B (p70) Jazz, jam sessions, indie gigs, DJ sets and more.

Hot Five Jazz & Blues Club (p52) The hottest jazz club in town.

Top Tips for a Night Out

○ In typical southern style, nights begin late here. Bars don't really crank up until around 11pm and clubs take over when they close at 2am-ish.

○ Book concert and theatre tickets at least a week ahead to ensure decent seats.

Shopping

Shopping in Porto is very much a local experience, whether you are tasting port before selecting the perfect take-home bottle, nattering to the friendly senhora at an old-school grocery about the merits of tremoços *(lupin beans), or talking to resident artists and designers at pop-ups, galleries and concept stores.*

Food & Drink

Touriga (p73) David Ferreira uncorks the world of Portuguese wines and ports.

A Pérola Do Bolhão (p72) Time-warp grocery store with an eye-popping art nouveau facade.

Chocolateria Ecuador (p53) Sublime dark chocolate (including one made with port wine).

Oliva & Co (p52) Premium extra virgin olive oils from all over Portugal.

Loja das Conservas (p52) Taking *conservas* (canned fish) to a whole new level.

Garrafeira do Carmo (p95) For vintage port and high-quality wines at reasonable prices.

Arts & Crafts

Azulima (p72) Jazz up your home with the Portuguese *azulejos* (hand-painted tiles) sold here.

A Vida Portuguesa (p75) An ode to all things Portuguese, including Bordallo Pinheiro *andorinhas* (swallows).

águas furtadas (p72) Modish Portuguese fashion, design and crafts.

Armazém (p95) Riverside warehouse turned concept and vintage store.

CRU (p115) Imaginative Portuguese crafts from a new wave of creatives.

Loja das Tábuas (p53) Cork products and oak *tábuas* (chopping boards).

Gifts

Coração Alecrim (p72) One-off retro, vintage and eco-friendly gifts in a delightful store.

Tradições (p53) Ribeira one-stop shop, with original finds from cork bags to *azulejos*.

Claus Porto (p53) Retro-wrapped luxury Portuguese soaps.

Vista Alegre (p73) Highly regarded Portuguese porcelain.

43 Branco (p53) Porto-inspired gifts from filigree jewellery to ceramic sardines.

Zinda Atelier (p52) Original ceramics, including Portugal's famous *andorinhas* (swallows), in a working studio.

INGEHOGENBIJL // SHUTTERSTOCK ©

Design & Fashion

Workshops Pop Up (p71) Original interior design and fashion buys.

Nuno Baltazar (p133) Flagship of the Portuguese catwalk king.

Monseo (p121) Jewellery funked up with Portuguese motifs.

Scar-id (p95) Some 40 designers show their work at this modern concept store.

Markets

Mercado Beira-Rio (p103) A covered food market that will get you up close and personal with *tripeiros* (porto residents).

Mercado da Foz (p141) With stalls piled high with fresh produce and flowers.

Mercado da Afurada (p109) Small but lively fish market in the pretty village of Afurada.

Mercado Bom Sucesso (p130) Offering everything from fresh food to concerts to courses.

The Best Shopping Streets

Click into the city's creative pulse along Rua Miguel Bombarda, home to a seemingly ever-expanding crop of art galleries, vintage shops and kooky boutiques. Mosey down Rua das Flores for all-Portuguese souvenirs worth showing off, or, for high-street stores, hit Rua de Santa Catarina.

Festivals & Events

Let's face it: the tripeiros need little excuse for a party, whether they are whacking each other with squeaky hammers at the riotous Festa de São João, celebrating São Pedro da Afurada by scoffing sardines, drinking vinho and dancing till dawn, or bopping to rock at open-air festivals in the sweet nights of summer. The more the merrier is the attitude in this high-spirited city.

DE VISU / SHUTTERSTOCK ©

Cultural & Heritage Events

Serralves Em Festa (www. serralves.pt) Runs for 50 hours nonstop over one weekend in early June. Parque de Serralves hosts the main events, with concerts, avant-garde theatre and kiddie activities.

Festival Internacional de Teatro de Expressão Ibérica (www.fitei.com) Celebrates contemporary theatre in Spanish and Portuguese. It's held over 10 days in mid-June.

Fantasporto (www.fantas porto.com) Two-week festival celebrating fantasy, horror and just plain weird films in February/March.

Queima das Fitas (www. queimadoporto.com) Parades, concerts, shows and round-the-clock partying at this shindig marking the end of the academic year.

Music Festivals

NOS Primavera Sound (www.nosprimaverasound. com) Rock, pop, electro and indie acts headline this festival at Porto's Parque da Cidade in early June.

MEO Marés Vivas (p108) Vila Nova de Gaia plays host to this big-name, three-day rock and pop festival in late July.

Noites Ritual Rock (www. facebook.com/pg/festival noitesritual) Free weekend-long rock bash at the Jardins do Palácio de Cristal.

Make it a Date: Must-Sees

○ Porto's wildest all-singing, all-dancing she-bang revolves around the celebration of the Santos Populares (Popular Saints) in June.

○ Join in the midsummer madness at Porto's biggest bash, the Festa de São João (pictured; p48), in June.

○ Afurada reels in the crowds parades, parties and sardine feasting at Festa de São Pedro da Afurada (p108) around 29 June.

Port Wine

You can't say you've been to Porto until you've tasted the Douro's oak-barrel-aged nectar and learned to tell a mellow, nutty tawny from a complex, sophisticated vintage. Since the 17th century, the swanky lodges spilling down Vila Nova de Gaia's hillside have been the nerve centre of port production.

SOHADISZNO / GETTY IMAGES ©

Cellar Tours

Taylor's (p100) Multilingual audioguide tours include a tasting of two top-of-the-range port wines. Fabulous views.

Graham's (p100) Perched high above the Douro, this lodge offers great insight into port production, concluding with a tasting.

Cálem (p100) Award-winning cellars with guided tours and tastings.

Ramos Pinto (p102) Down by the river, with cellars, tours and tastings.

Croft (p102) Going strong since 1588, this rustically elegant lodge carved out of the hillside has tastings.

Sandeman (p100) Guides in black capes lead you through Sandeman's centuries-old cellars.

Tasting & Shopping

Prova (p51) Chic, relaxed bar with tastings.

Portologia (p51) Cosy wine bar with 200 different ports on offer and tastings.

Touriga (p73) A trove of well- and lesser-known ports and wines. Offers tastings, too.

Garrafeira do Carmo (p95) Take your pick from a mind-boggling array of ports at this central store.

Experiences

Douro Azul (p101) Drift along the Douro in replica *barcos rabelos*, flat-bottomed boats that once transported wine from the vineyards.

Espaço Porto Cruz (p99) A contemporary ode to port wine in a historic building, with a museum, restaurant, tastings and terrace.

For Free

There's so much to discover in Porto without spending a cent. Sunset city views from hilltop miradouros, botanical garden strolls, swims in the nearby Atlantic and walks in the alley-woven historic centre – all free, free and free again. You can see everything from cutting-edge photography to baroque churches smothered in azulejos gratis in this astonishingly good-value city.

EMILY MCAULIFFE / LONELY PLANET ©

Weekend Cent Savers

With a little careful timing, you can considerably slash the costs of exploring Porto. Save sightseeing for the weekend. Big-hitter museums, you say? Head over to the cutting-edge Serralves (p136), which opens its doors for free on the first Sunday morning of the month. And the Museu Romântico (p117) is free all weekend long.

Free Sights

São Bento Train Station (p60) Rewind back to rail travel's glory days and bone up on Portuguese history admiring *azulejos*.

Capela das Almas (pictured; p60) Extraordinary *azulejo*-adorned church, with panels spelling out the lives of saints.

Centro Português de Fotografia (p82) Zoom in on cutting-edge photography at this former prison.

Sé (p34) Porto's crowning glory cathedral is a fortified Romanesque giant with sweeping city views.

Igreja do Carmo (p88) Stunning *azulejo*-clad church, with a frieze on the facade paying homage to Nossa Senhora (Our Lady).

Free Outdoors

Jardins do Palácio de Cristal (p112) A botanical beauty with sky-high views of Porto.

Ponte de Dom Luís I (p44) Walk the upper level of this double-decker bridge for knockout views, emerging at the Jardim do Morro.

Foz do Douro (p135) Explore a fort, stroll a seafront promenade and paddle in the Atlantic.

Jardim do Morro (p99) Pretty gardens in Gaia with spirit-lifting views of the historic centre.

Parque da Cidade (p143) A mammoth lake-dotted park, complete with cycling and walking trails.

Tours

To see the city from a more personal angle, hook onto one of Porto's guided tours. These swing from half-day foodie rambles to cruises taking you to Douro Valley vineyards and insightful themed tours homing in on everything from azulejos to urban art and Jewish heritage. Or, if you fancy something more active, you can buzz about town on a bike or Vespa.

JOYFULL / SHUTTERSTOCK ©

Food Tours & Cookery Courses

Taste Porto (p66) On-the-ball tours of the city's food and drink scene.

Workshops Pop Up (p71) Learn to cook Portuguese classics and feast on the fruits of your labour.

Walking, Bike & Tuk-Tuk Tours

Tuk Tour (p62) Get around the city and beyond by tuk-tuk.

Fold 'n' Visit (p149) Bike rentals and cycling tours of downtown Porto.

Worst Tours (www.the worsttours.weebly.com; Praça do Marquês de Pom-

bal) Free and fun offbeat tours of Porto on foot.

Porto Walkers (p62) Young, sparky guides showing you their side of the city.

Living Tours (p46) City tours and trips further afield to Douro and Minho.

Oporto Share (p45) Zip around town on a guided Vespa tour.

Themed Tours

Other Side (p45) Discover Porto's hidden nooks on themed tours, or venture to the Douro vineyards.

Porto Sky Experience (p118) Get an aerial angle on Porto in a helicopter.

Blue Dragon Tours (p45) Themed walking, cycling and Segway tours.

Be My Guest (p103) Quirky, insidery tours covering everything from *azulejos* to urban art.

eFun GPS tours (p102) From historic centre walks to Jewish heritage tours.

Boat Tours

Barcadouro (Map p98, C2; ☎223 722 415; www. barcadouro.pt; Av Ramos Pinto 240, Cais de Gaia, Vila Nova de Gaia) Day trip it to the Douro Valley by boat.

Douro Acima (p46) Short cruises along the Douro in *barcos rabelos*.

Douro Azul (p101) Multi-lingual 50-minute river cruises.

Outdoors

CRISTIAN BALATE / SHUTTERSTOCK ©

Whether it is the river glimpsed wistfully from miradouros *(viewpoints), a sunset snapshot of the city as seen from a lush botanical garden, or a reviving walk or bike ride along the seafront or through the city's biggest park, Porto effortlessly combines the urban with the outdoors. And the heart of Douro wine country is also on the city's doorstep.*

Ocean breezes, a plentiful supply of Atlantic-fresh fish and the caw of seagulls are reminders that Porto is a city shaped by the sea. Foz do Douro's promenade and beaches are just a short hop from the centre, so you can easily tie in a morning's sightseeing with an afternoon spent here. Even better beaches lie further north in Vila do Conde, an hour's trundle away on the B (red) metro line.

Parks & Gardens

Jardins do Palácio de Cristal (p112) The Porto views are uplifting from these hilltop botanical gardens.

Jardim da Cordoaria (pictured; p89) Sculptures, shade and trams rattling on by in this central garden.

Jardim do Passeio Alegre (p139) A pretty promenade for a Sunday stroll beside the seaside in Foz.

Jardim Botânico do Porto (p127) Wander among the lakes and flowers at these cool, tucked-away gardens.

Parque da Cidade (p143) Walk, cycle or go for a picnic in Porto's biggest green space.

Viewpoints

Miradouro da Vitória (p85) Dusk is prime time to see the city illuminated from this Vitória viewpoint.

Torre dos Clérigos (p60) Clamber up this tower for views reaching to the Douro and beyond.

Porto Bridge Climb (p118) Pluck up the nerve to scale Ponte da Arrábida for giddy river and city views.

Jardim do Morro (p99) Hilltop gardens with cracking Douro and Ribeira views.

Jardim das Virtudes (p88) These terraced gardens overlooking Porto's rooftops are a much-loved local hang-out.

Art & Architecture

Beyond Porto's historic heart, contemporary architects have left their imprint on crisply minimalist buildings that strike a perfect balance with their often-natural surrounds. Winging the city into the 21st century, local Pritzker Prize–winning architects Álvaro Siza Vieira and Eduardo Souto de Moura are the dream duo. Public art adds an element of interest to the every day.

EMILY MCAULIFFE / LONELY PLANET ©

Historic Highs

Sé (p34) Porto's fortress-like Romanesque cathedral has Gothic and baroque touches.

São Bento Train Station (p60) A romantic, *azulejo*-clad edifice in beaux arts style.

Palácio da Bolsa (p38) Austerely neoclassical on the outside, Porto's former stock exchange hides exquisite interiors.

Avenida dos Aliados (pictured; p60) The grand and the glorious buildings that line this avenue present a roll call of architectural styles – from neoclassical to French beaux arts.

Igreja de São Francisco (p36) A lavishly gilded baroque treat.

Street Art

Rua das Flores (p74) Vibrant works by Hazul, glowing neon portraits by Costah and 15 electric boxes – each with its own burst of street-art colour.

Rua Miguel Bombarda (p114) Gallery dotted and street-art splashed.

Cutting-Edge Architecture

Casa da Música (p124) Porto's iconic Rem Koolhaas–designed concert hall takes acoustics to another dimension.

Serralves (p136) An angular, whitewashed Álvaro Siza Vieira–designed gallery, set in parkland and amplifying light and space.

Boa Nova Tea House (p143) A clifftop stunner overlooking the ocean by starchitect Vieira.

Taking a Self-Guided Tour

○ Get inspiration for your own self-guided tour of Porto's hottest contemporary architecture with the free maps guides hand out at the tourist office.

For Kids

Exploring Porto with tots (or teenagers) can be child's play with a little know-how. What could be more kid-friendly, after all, than screeching through the streets on a vintage tram, devising your very own Harry Potter trail in the city that once inspired JK Rowling's magical pen, hitting the beaches in Foz, or finding adventure in the footsteps of great Portuguese navigators?

HERACLES KRITIKOS / SHUTTERSTOCK ©

Hands-On Fun

Sealife Porto (p143) Kids can watch sharks glide overhead, handle starfish and find Nemo at this whopper of an aquarium.

Museu das Marionetas (p88) Puppets on strings are in the spotlight at this marionette museum.

World of Discoveries (pictured; p117) Slip into the shoes of a swashbuckling explorer at this discovery-focused sight.

Look at Porto (p117) Take a virtual flight over Porto at this 5D cinema.

Art & Inspiration

Serralves (p136) Check out the activity-driven family weekend workshops.

Ponte de Dom Luís I (p44) Budding photographers can practise snapping Porto's ginormous bridge.

Livraria Lello (p60) More than a pinch of Potter...

Rua das Flores (p74) Give them a scrapbook for a self-guided street art tour.

Outdoors

Foz do Douro (p135) Hop aboard tram 1 to Foz for ice cream, lighthouse snapshots and beach fun.

Jardins do Palácio de Cristal (p112) Porto is reduced to pop-up-book scale from these glorious gardens complete with peacocks.

Parque da Cidade (p143) Kids love letting off steam in Porto's biggest park. Perfect for a picnic.

Top Tips for Family Savings

- Kids under four travel free on public transport.

- Museums are free or discounted for under-14s or under-18s.

- Some restaurants have kids' menus or offer a *meia dose* (half-portion).

Museums & Galleries

Dipping into Porto's museums gives you insight into how the city has been shaped by the past and what makes it tick today. Some are small and intimate, focusing on special interests from photography to puppets, while others are much grander affairs, housed in stately palaces or minimalist buildings on the cutting-edge of cool.

TRABANTOS / SHUTTERSTOCK ©

Ancient & Contemporary Art

Museu Nacional Soares dos Reis (p80) Porto's must-see art museum is a spectacular romp through fine and decorative arts.

Museu da Misericórdia do Porto (p44) Avant-garde architecture merges seamlessly with sacred art.

Serralves (p136) Contemporary art from the 1960s to the present day.

Special Interest

Centro Português de Fotografia (p82) Zoom into today's photography scene at this born-again prison.

Museu dos Transportes (p89) Trace cars, radio and telecommunications back to their roots in this grand 19th-century customs house.

Museu do Carro Eléctrico (p118) Love Porto's trams? This one is for you, with its stellar collection of vintage numbers.

Museu das Marionetas (p88) Find out who pulls the strings of the marionettes at this family-friendly museum.

Heritage

Casa do Infante (p44) Henry the Navigator, Age of Discovery superstar, was born in Porto's first customs house in 1394.

Museu Romântico (p117) This fine romance of a museum is where the exiled king of Sardinia spent his final days.

Palácio da Bolsa (pictured; p38) Revealing the wealth of the city's former money-bags.

Making the Most of Your Visit

○ Most museums and sights close on Mondays, and some offer free admission at least one morning at the weekend.

○ Most museums and sights don't permit photography (at least with a flash). Ask first.

Four Perfect Days

Day 1

ARKADY ZARKAROV / SHUTTERSTOCK ©

Begin with knockout views of historic Porto from the fortress-like **Sé** (pictured; p34). From here, dive into Ribeira's knot of alleys, which spill down a hillside. Stop at the **Museu da Misericórdia** (p44) for a culture shot and glimpse at the church's extraordinary *azulejos*. Dedicate the afternoon to Ribeira's biggest crowd-pullers. First up is the **Igreja de São Francisco** (p36), which packs a glitzy baroque punch. Equally sumptuous is the nearby neoclassical **Palácio da Bolsa** (p38) – hook onto one of its whirlwind guided tours. As the sun sets over the Rio Douro, snag a table at **Wine Quay Bar** (p51) for predinner drinks with a view of the graceful swoop of **Ponte de Dom Luís I** (p44).

Day 2

FOTONON / SHUTTERSTOCK ©

Explore fin-de-siècle **São Bento** (p60) train station, where *azulejo* panels recount Porto's history. From here, the beaux arts style **Avenida dos Aliados** (p60) swaggers north. Pop into old-school grocery stores along Rua de Sá da Bandeira, then meander **Rua de Santa Catarina** (p57) to Capela das Almas. Grab a coffee at **Café Majestic** (p68) or a *francesinha* at **Cafe Santiago** (p63). Devote your afternoon to a walking tour with **Taste Porto** (p66) or head to **Torre dos Clérigos** (p60) for knockout city views and neo-Gothic bookstore **Livraria Lello** (pictured; p60). Book a table for dinner at urban-hip **MUU** (p65) or gourmet **Euskalduna Studio** (p65), before hitting some of the DJ-driven bars around the Galerias – Porto's party central.

Day 3

EMILY MCAULIFFE / LONELY PLANET ©

Go for a creative brunch at **Época** (pictured; p89), before taking in Miragaia's sights. Photography buffs: turn to **Centro Português de Fotografia** (p82), then take a leisurely mooch around the former Jewish quarter's *azulejo*-tiled, street-art-splashed medieval lanes, pausing for views from **Miradouro da Vitória** (p85). Have lunch at family-run **Taberna de Santo António** (p85) then cut north through the **Jardim da Cordoaria** (p89) to **Museu Nacional Soares dos Reis** (p80), a top-drawer collection of fine and decorative arts. One street over is gallery-dotted **Rua Miguel Bombarda** (p114). Round out the afternoon in **Jardins do Palácio de Cristal** (p112) and uplifting views and predinner drinks at **Miradouro Ignez** (p120).

Day 4

EMILY MCAULIFFE / LONELY PLANET ©

That bridge you keep seeing? It's time to walk across **Ponte de Dom Luís I** (p44) to **Jardim do Morro** (p99). Swing down to Vila Nova de Gaia's waterfront in the cable car, then hit **Taylor's** (p100) or **Graham's** (p100) for a port cellar tour and tasting with views. Treat yourself to lunch at **Vinum** (p105). From Ribeira, take the tram to Foz do Douro, a tonic to the buzz of the city, with its promenade, gardens and beachfront cafes, including **Praia da Luz** (p140). Go for a coffee at **The Bird** (p139) then head down to the seafront. Follow dinner at the sensational **Boa Nova Tea House** (pictured; p143) – book ahead – with drinks at ship-shape **Bonaparte** (p140).

Need to Know

For detailed information, see Survival Guide (p144)

Currency
Euro (€)

Language
Portuguese

Visas
EU nationals need no visa. US, Canadian, Australian and New Zealand visitors can stay for up to 90 days without a visa.

Money
ATMs widely available. Credit cards generally accepted. Cash preferred in some small shops and restaurants.

Mobile Phones
GSM and 4G networks available. EU nationals can 'roam like at home' at no extra charge. Other travellers can save by buying a local SIM.

Time
Porto is on GMT/UTC.

Tipping
Service is not usually added to the bill. Tip an average of 10% if you are satisfied.

Daily Budget

Budget: Less than €60
Dorm bed: €18–25
Double room in a budget hotel: €40–60
Lunch special with drink: €10
Single ticket on the metro: €1.20–2

Midrange: €60–150
Double room in a central hotel: €60–120
Meal in a midrange restaurant: €20–30
Guided half-day bike tour: from €17
Tour of a port cellar including tasting: €5–10

Top end: More than €150
Double room in a boutique hotel: from €100
Three-course dinner with wine: from €40
Theatre/concert tickets: €15–30
Full-day tour of the Douro: €90

Advance Planning

One month before Book hotel rooms (if you haven't already), festival, theatre and concert tickets, and excursions. Brush up on your Portuguese.

Two weeks before Reserve a table at the city's top restaurants.

A few days before Check out what's happening on events websites (www.visit porto.travel is a good first port of call). Get versed in the subtle nuances of port wine – the Taylor's website (www.taylor.pt/en) gives an overview.

Arriving in Porto

Most travellers will arrive in Porto via air. The airport is located around 16km northwest of the city centre. It's roughly a 45-minute journey to downtown Porto.

✈ Francisco Sá Carneiro Airport

Metro Line E (direction Estádio do Dragão) links the airport to downtown Porto, 6am to 1am, €2

Bus Bus 601 to Cordoaria, 5.30am to 11.30pm, €2

Taxi 24 hours, rank outside Arrivals, €20 to €25

✈ At the Airport

Porto's gleaming Francisco Sá Carneiro Airport (p147) is modern and easy to navigate. It has numerous cafes, bars, restaurants and shops, as well as a post office, ATMs, baby-changing facilities, car rental, left luggage and a tourist information point. The first 30 minutes of wi-fi is free for passengers.

Getting Around

Public transport is inexpensive and efficient. Buy the rechargeable Andante Card (€0.60), allowing smooth movement between tram, metro, funicular and many bus lines. For timetables, routes and fares, see www.stcp.pt.

Ⓜ Metro

Porto's six-line metro network runs from 6am to 1am daily. Tickets cost €1.20/1.60/2 for zone 2/3/4. See www.metrodoporto.pt for details and maps.

🚃 Tram

Three lines, every 30 minutes from 8am to 9pm. One-way tickets cost €3.

🚌 Bus

Extensive but slow. One-way tickets cost €1.95 when purchased on board, €1.20 with an Andante Card.

🚕 Taxi

Costs around €5 to €7 for short trips. Taxi ranks in centre or call 225 076 400.

Porto Neighbourhoods

Boavista (p123)
Porto goes 21st century with cutting-edge architecture in Boavista, where the avenue of the same name leads to the crashing Atlantic.

Serralves ⊙

Casa da Música ⊙

Foz do Douro & Around (p135)
This seafront neighbourhood has its own appeal, with gardens, parks and esplanades for strolling, a string of beaches, a lighthouse and a castle emphasising big Atlantic views.

⊙ Afurada

Massarelos (p111)
Sidestep the tourist trail in this offbeat neighbourhood, with botanical gardens, a sprinkling of sights and family-run restaurants.

Miragaia (p79)
History seeps through this alley-woven district, with stellar museums, low-key streets bubbling with local life and a rich Jewish heritage.

Aliados & Bolhão (p55)
Go back in time at old-school grocers and market halls, then ramp up the urban-cool factor at happening boutiques and bars.

Ribeira (p33)
Crowned by a hefty cathedral and lined with shops, bars and restaurants that spill picturesquely down to the Rio Douro.

Jardins do Palácio de Cristal ◉

◉ Museu Nacional Soares dos Reis

Centro Português de Fotografia ◉

Palácio da Bolsa

◉ Sé

◉ Igreja de São Francisco

Vila Nova de Gaia (p97)
Teasing glimpses of the river and port-wine tastings are yours for the savouring in this neighbourhood.

Explore
Porto

Worth a Trip 👀

Porto's Walking Tours 🥾

Rua de Santa Catarina (p57) TRABANTOS / SHUTTERSTOCK ©

Explore

Ribeira

Ribeira is Porto's biggest heart-stealer. Its Unesco World Heritage maze of medieval alleys zigzags down a promenade straddling the Douro River, with front-row views of the spectacular Ponte de Dom Luís I and the port-wine lodges across the river in Vila Nova de Gaia. Jam-packed with sights, shops and restaurants (and flocks of tourists), this historic neighbourhood is postcard Porto.

Begin at the Sé (p34), Porto's fortified Romanesque cathedral, lording it above the medieval alleys of the Unesco World Heritage historic centre. Particularly pretty is Rua das Flores, home to the outstanding Museu da Misericórdia do Porto (p44), pavement cafes and speciality shops. Tour the lavish Palácio da Bolsa (p38) before turning the corner to Igreja de São Francisco (p36), which bombards you with its gilded baroque splendour.

As evening approaches, amble down to bar-lined Cais da Ribeira (p44) as the iconic Ponte de Dom Luís I lights up. Book a table for dinner at Cantina 32 (p48) for creative takes on petiscos (small plates), or head to Prova (p51) for fine wines and smooth jazz.

Getting There & Around

Ⓜ **Metro** The local stop is São Bento (yellow metro line D).

🚋 **Tram** Tram 1 runs along the river, linking the historic centre to Passeio Alegre in Foz. It stops on the Rua Nova da Alfândega in front of the Igreja de São Francisco.

Ribeira Map on p42

Ribeira Map on p42

Aerial view of Ribeira JOYFULL / SHUTTERSTOCK ©

Top Sight 📷

Sé

Rising high and mighty above Porto's tangle of medieval alleys and stairways, this hulking, hilltop fortress of a 12th-century cathedral was given a baroque makeover in the 18th century. History, however, lends it gravitas – this is where Prince Henry the Navigator was baptised in 1394 and where King John I married his beloved Philippa of Lancaster in 1387.

◎ MAP P42, E3

Terreiro da Sé

cloisters adult/student €3/2

🕙 9am-7pm Apr-Oct, to 6pm Nov-Mar

Facade

Located strategically on a hillside, the cathedral is visible from afar. The terrace grants sweeping views that reach over the historic centre's lanes and rooftops and down to the Douro. Carved from local granite, the facade resembles a fortress with its pair of sturdy towers and crenellations. You can still make out its Romanesque contours.

Interior

The Romanesque barrel-vaulted nave and the Gothic rose window recall the cathedral's earlier origins. Keep an eye out for the baroque altarpiece in the Chapel of the Holy Sacrament, exquisitely wrought from silver; the Gothic funerary chapel of João Gordo, a Knight Hospitaller for King Dinis I; and Portuguese sculptor António Teixeira Lopes' bronze bas-relief depicting Christ's baptism by John the Baptist.

Cloister & Loggia

Blue and white *azulejos* (hand-painted tiles) dating from the 18th century and evoking scenes from the Song of Solomon dance elegantly across the walls of the Gothic cloister, a peaceful spot for a contemplative stroll. The baroque loggia by Italian architect Nicolau Nasoni is adorned with more beautiful 18th-century tiles by Valentim de Almeida, which show the life of the Virgin Mary.

Courtyards

There are several treasures in the cathedral courtyards. Look out for a barley-twist neo-Pombaline pillary and the Chafariz de São Miguel, an 18th-century fountain by Nasoni topped with a little statue of St Michael the Archangel. In the grounds, notice too the grand baroque facade of the Paço Episcopal, former residence of the bishops of Porto.

★ Top Tips

o Come to the cathedral as day softens into dusk for photogenic views of the Old Town and river.

o Dip into the maze of surrounding alleyways for a serendipitous wander.

o Attend one of the services – 11am mass on Sunday and 7pm evensong daily.

✗ Take a Break

Go for coffee, homemade cakes or breakfast at the nearby Mercado Café (p48).

Wander down the long flight of steps to Ribeira's riverfront for a tapas lunch at Jimão (p49).

Top Sight 📷
Igreja de São Francisco

Igreja de São Francisco looks for all the world like an austerely Gothic church from the outside, but inside it hides one of Portugal's most dazzling displays of baroque finery. Hardly a centimetre escapes unsmothered, as otherworldly cherubs and sober monks are drowned by nearly 100kg of gold leaf. If you only see one church in Porto, make it this one.

◎ MAP P42, B5

Jardim do Infante Dom Henrique

adult/child €6/5

🕒 9am-8pm Jul-Sep, to 7pm Mar-Jun & Oct, to 5.30pm Nov-Feb

The Nave

The church's nave should be high on your list, interwoven with vines and curlicues, dripping with cherubs and shot through with gold leaf. Peel back the layers to find standouts such as the Manueline-style Chapel of St John the Baptist and the 13th-century statue of St Francis of Assisi.

Tree of Jesse

The handiwork of master craftsmen Filipe da Silva and António Gomes, this polychrome marvel of an altarpiece (1718 and 1721) traces the genealogy of Christ. The tree roots grow from the loins of a reclining Jesse of Bethlehem at the base up into branches with the 12 kings of Judah. In a niche is the Virgin Mary and infant Jesus.

Church Museum

Opposite the church, the museum harbours a fine, well-edited collection of sacred art. Besides portraits of bishops in all their ecclesiastical finery, there are some beautiful baroque altarpieces, tabernacles, silverware and ceramics. On the ground floor of the museum, one of the star pieces is a 1799 painting of St Louis, King of France, by famous Porto-born artist Vieira Portuense.

Catacombs

In the eerily atmospheric catacombs, the great and the good of Porto were once buried; in fact, all Portuguese were buried in churches before 1845 as public cemeteries did not exist. Tiptoe past the headstones, looking out for sculptural works by Italian master Nicolau Nasoni and prolific Portuguese sculptor António Teixeira Lopes. The ossuary is a spine-tingling work of art.

★ Top Tips

o Tram 1 stops right in front of the church. Hop aboard it and you can be beside the sea in Foz do Douro within minutes.

o Leave digicams and smartphones behind – photography is not permitted.

o To see the church at its quiet best, rise early to be there as it opens, or come in early evening in summer.

✕ Take a Break

Snag a table on the terrace at nearby Bacalhau (p50) for cracking river views as you chomp on *petiscos* (tapas) or creative takes on codfish.

For traditional Portuguese grub, mooch over to A Grade (p50), where the seafood is super-fresh and the welcome warm.

Ribeira Igreja de São Francisco

Top Sight 📷
Palácio da Bolsa

One glimpse at Porto's lavish Palácio da Bolsa tells you precisely who once held the purse strings. Built from 1842 to 1910, the splendid neoclassical stock exchange honours Porto's past and present money merchants. Its halls are replete with exquisite murals, mosaics and artworks.

◎ MAP P42, A5

Stock Exchange

www.palaciodabolsa.com

Rua Ferreira Borges

tours adult/child €9/5.50

🕑 9am-6.30pm Apr-Oct, 9am-12.30pm & 2-5.30pm Nov-Mar

Salão Árabe

The palace's crowning glory is the stupendous Arabian Hall, with stucco teased into complex Moorish designs, then gilded with some 20kg of gold. Inspired by the Alhambra in Granada, Spain, it has arabesques dancing across its polychrome walls and columns rising gracefully to keyhole arches and stained-glass windows. No surface is left untouched.

Pátio das Nações

The Hall of Nations is the first thing you see as you enter – and it's a stunner. Lit by an octagonal skylight, this courtyard is where the exchange operated. You'll see the coat of arms of Portugal and the countries with which it once traded, and the Greco-Roman floor mosaic inspired by Pompeii.

Gabinete de Gustave Eiffel

This simply furnished study is where that famous French civil engineer architect Gustave Eiffel beavered away from 1875 to 1877, the Eiffel Tower then but a Parisian twinkle in his eye. The study has a view of the Ponte de Dom Luís I, but it is the Ponte Maria Pia, just out of sight, that bears his hallmark.

Escadaria Noble

Beautifully wrought in granite, the Noble Staircase took 68 years to complete because it was so hard to carve. Look for the busts of feted sculptors António Soares dos Reis and António Teixeira Lopes, a pair of striking bronze chandeliers and the ceiling frescoes by António Ramalho.

Sala do Tribunal

You can feel the weight of history in this grand courtroom, with its ornately carved wooden benches and vivid murals showing the wealth of commercial activity in the city and region. To this day, this is where port is declared 'vintage'.

★ Top Tips

○ Hook onto one of the half-hour guided tours, which set off every 30 minutes.

○ In the Sala dos Retratos (Portrait Hall), take a peek at the intricate table, which took engraver Zeferino José Pinto three years to carve with a pocket knife.

○ Tie in a visit with a wine tasting at **ViniPortugal** (Map p42, B5; www.vini portugal.pt/ogival rooms; 🕑11am-7pm Mon-Sat Apr-Oct, 2-7pm Mon-Sat Nov-Mar).

🍴 Take a Break

Linger in palatial splendour over lunch or dinner at **O Comercial** (Map p42, B5; 📞918 838 649; www.ocomercial.com; 3-course set lunch/dinner €17/23; 🕑12.30-3pm & 7.30-10.30pm Mon-Fri, 7.30-11.30pm Sat), serving Med-style flavours with a touch of class.

It's a quick walk to Ode Porto Wine House (p51) for slow food and Portuguese wines.

Walking Tour 🥾

Porto's Unesco World Heritage Heart

Rising in a helter-skelter of chalk-bright houses, soaring bell towers and Gothic and baroque churches, Porto's Unesco-listed historic heart is a dream of medieval loveliness made for strolling. Cobblestone streets twist past old curiosity shops and pavement cafes that hum with local gossip, and every so often the cityscape cracks open to reveal miradouros (viewpoints) over Porto.

Walk Facts

Start Igreja da Misericórdia

End Ponte de Dom Luís I

Length 4km; four hours

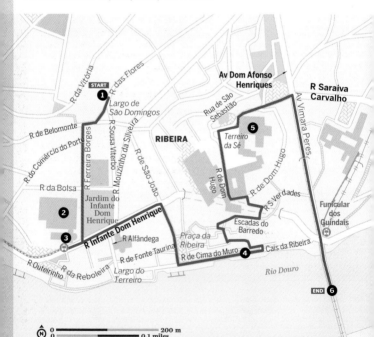

❶ Museu da Misericórdia do Porto

Duck down Rua das Flores, one of Ribeira's most charming streets, lined with delis, cafes, boutiques and speciality shops, and splashed with vibrant street art. To the right near the bottom sits the **Museu da Misericórdia do Porto** (p44), a baroque beauty designed by Nicolau Nasoni, with an interior replete with blue-and-white *azulejos*.

❷ Palácio da Bolsa

A mosey down Rua Ferreira Borges brings you to the Jardim do Infante Dom Henrique, flanked by the late-19th-century Mercado Ferreira Borges market hall and the neoclassical grandeur of the **Palácio da Bolsa** (p38). Henry the Navigator stands high on a pedestal at the centre of the square.

❸ Igreja de São Francisco

Swinging a right brings you to the Jardim do Infante Dom Henrique and the **Igreja de São Francisco** (p36), Porto's most sublime church: Gothic on the outside and a feast of over-the-top, gilded baroque splendour on the inside.

❹ Cais da Ribeira

Strolling along **Cais da Ribeira** (p44) is your golden ticket to the city's soul. This is Porto of a million postcards – the Ribeira's chalk-hued houses rising behind you, the Rio Douro unfurling before you, street entertainers serenading you. Colourful *barcos rabelos* (flat-bottomed boats) bob in front of pavement cafes and restaurants, and the graceful swoop of the Ponte de Dom Luís I frames the picture neatly.

❺ Sé

Take a steep flight of steps uphill from the river to Porto's crowning glory, the fortresslike **cathedral** (p34). History reverberates in its Romanesque-meets-baroque nave and cloister, and the terrace commands photogenic views of the cityscape.

❻ Ponte de Dom Luís I

Exit right onto Calçada de Vandoma, then veer right again onto Avenida Vimara Peres, which will bring you to that whopper of a double-decker arched bridge, the **Ponte de Dom Luís I** (p44), taking a spectacular leap over the Douro. Cross it for swoon-worthy views, keeping your eye out for daredevils jumping off its lower level.

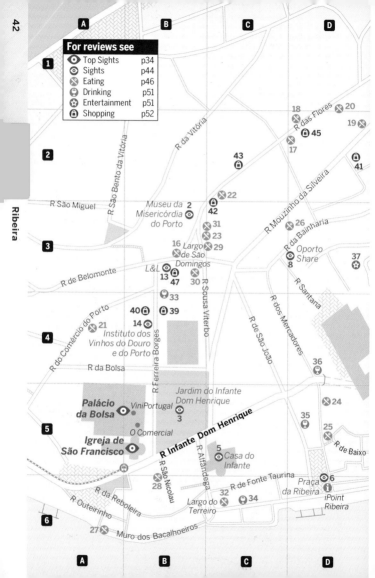

Ribeira

For reviews see
- ◉ Top Sights   p34
- ⊙ Sights   p44
- ✗ Eating   p46
- 🍷 Drinking   p51
- ✪ Entertainment p51
- 🛍 Shopping   p52

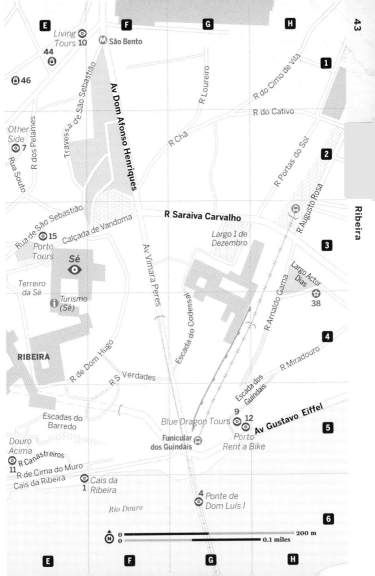

Ribeira

E

E
44
46
Other Side 7
Rua Souto
R dos Pelames

F
Living Tours 10
M São Bento
Travessa de São Sebastião

G

H
R do Cimo de Vila
R do Cativo

1

R Loureiro
R Cha

R Portas do Sol

2

Rua de São Sebastião
Porto Tours 15
Calçada de Vandoma

R Saraiva Carvalho

Largo 1 de Dezembro

R Augusto Rosa

3

Sé
Terreiro da Sé
Turismo (Sé)

Av Vimara Peres

Largo Actor Dias
38

R Arnaldo Gama

4

RIBEIRA

R de Dom Hugo
R S Verdades

Escada do Codessal

R Miradouro
Escada dos Guindais

Escadas do Barredo

Blue Dragon Tours
Funicular dos Guindais

9 12
Porto Rent a Bike

Av Gustavo Eiffel

5

Douro Acima
11
R Canastreiros
R de Cima do Muro
Cais da Ribeira

Cais da Ribeira 1

4 Ponte de Dom Luís I

Rio Douro

6

N 0
0

200 m
0.1 miles

E

F

G

H

Sights

Cais da Ribeira
AREA

1 ⊙ MAP P42, E6

This riverfront promenade is postcard Porto, taking in the whole spectacular sweep of the city, from Ribeira's pastel houses stacked like Lego bricks to the *barcos rabelos* (flat-bottomed boats) once used to transport port from the Douro. Early-evening buskers serenade crowds, and chefs fire up grills in the hole-in-the-wall fish restaurants and *tascas* (taverns) in the old arcades.

Museu da Misericórdia do Porto
CHURCH, MUSEUM

2 ⊙ MAP P42, B3

The Museu da Misericórdia do Porto harmoniously unites cutting-edge architecture, a prized collection of 15th- to 17th-century sacred art and portraiture, and one of Ribeira's finest churches, Igreja da Misericórdia. Bearing the hallmark of Italian baroque architect Nicolau Nasoni, the church's interior is adorned with blue-and-white *azulejos* (hand-painted tiles). The museum's biggest stunner is the large-scale Flemish Renaissance painting *Fons Vitae* (Fountain of Life), depicting Dom Manuel I and family around a fountain of blood from the crucified Christ. (MMIPO; www.mmipo.pt; Rua das Flores 5; adult/child €5/2.50; ☉10am-6.30pm Apr-Sep, to 5.30pm Oct-Mar)

Jardim do Infante Dom Henrique
GARDENS

3 ⊙ MAP P42, B5

Presided over by the late-19th-century market hall Mercado Ferreira Borges and neoclassical Palácio da Bolsa (p38), these gardens are named after the centre-piece statue. Lifted high on a pedestal, the monument depicts Prince Henry the Navigator (1394–1460) – a catalyst in the Age of Discoveries and pioneer of the caravel, who braved the battering Atlantic in search of colonies for Portugal's collection. (Rua Ferreira Borges)

Ponte de Dom Luís I
BRIDGE

4 ⊙ MAP P42, G5

Completed in 1886 by a student of Gustave Eiffel, the bridge's top deck is now reserved for pedestrians, as well as one of the city's metro lines; the lower deck bears regular traffic, as well as narrow walkways for those on foot. The views of the river and Old Town are simply stunning, as are the daredevils who leap from the lower level.

Casa do Infante
HISTORIC BUILDING

5 ⊙ MAP P42, C5

In this handsomely renovated medieval town house, according to legend, Henry the Navigator was born in 1394. The building later served as Porto's first customs house. Today it boasts three floors of exhibits. In 2002 the complex was excavated, revealing Roman foundations and some remarkable mosaics – all of which are now on display. (Rua Alfândega 10; adult/child €2.20/free; ⏰9.30am-1pm & 2-5.30pm Tue-Sun)

Praça da Ribeira
PLAZA

6 ◎ MAP P42, D6

Down by the Rio Douro, narrow streets open out onto a plaza framed by austerely grand, tiled town houses overlooking a picturesque stretch of the river. From here you have fine views of the port-wine lodges across the river as well as the monumental, double-decker Ponte de Dom Luís I.

Other Side
TOURS

7 ◎ MAP P42, E2

Well-informed, congenial guides reveal their city on half-day walking tours of hidden Porto (€19), a walking and food tour (€49), and wine tours (€55). They also venture further afield with full-day trips to the Douro's vineyards (€95), and to Guimarães and Braga (€85). (📞916 500 170; www.theotherside.pt; Rua Souto 67; ⏰9am-8pm)

Oporto Share
TOURS

8 ◎ MAP P42, D3

If you would rather buzz around Porto by Vespa than walk, Oporto Share offers nippy sightseeing tours by scooter. It also offers longer tours by minivan. (📞220 999 120; www.oportoshare.pt; Rua da Bainharia 20; tours from €20)

Blue Dragon Tours
TOURS

9 ◎ MAP P42, G5

This reputable outfit runs Old Town and riverside bike tours (€32.50), which make the link between the historic centre and the sea. It also offers several half-day walking tours, including the Best of Porto (€18) and a food and wine tour (€55), as well as two-hour Segway tours (€45) to tick off the highlights. Prices can depend on group sizes. (📞222 022 375; www.bluedragon.pt; Av Gustavo Eiffel 280; tours from €18)

Bridge over Troubled Waters

The construction of the Ponte de Dom Luís I over the Douro River was significant, as the area's foot traffic once travelled across a bridge made from old port boats lashed together. To make matters worse, the river was wild back then, with no upstream dams. When Napoleon invaded in 1809, scores were crushed and drowned in the rushing river as a panicked stampede proved too much for the makeshift bridge.

When the bridge was completed in 1886 by German architect Téophile Seyrig, who was an associate of Gustave Eiffel, it held the record for the longest iron arch in the world, with a span of 172m.

Living Tours TOURS

10 MAP P42, E1

A great range of sightseeing options are on offer at this friendly agency, from half-day city tours (€37.50) to fado tours with dinner (€70), and day trips to the Douro and Minho (€98). (228 320 992; www.livingtours.pt; Rua Mouzinho da Silveira 352-4; 9am-8pm Apr-Oct, to 6pm Nov-Mar)

Douro Acima BOATING

11 MAP P42, E5

Douro Acima runs 50-minute cruises along the Douro in *barcos rabelos*. There are departures every 30 minutes. (www.douroacima.pt; Rua dos Canastreiros 40; tours adult/child €15/7.50; 10am-6.30pm Apr-Oct, to 4.30pm Mar)

Porto Rent a Bike CYCLING

12 MAP P42, G5

Central-bike rental outlet. Besides city bikes, electric bikes, tandems and folding bikes are available. (912 562 190, 222 022 375; www.portorentabike.com; Av Gustavo Eiffel 280; bikes per half-/full day from €10/15; 10am-2pm & 3-7pm)

L&L CYCLING

13 MAP P42, B3

Bike rental in the heart of the Ribeira district. (223 251 722; www.lopesrentabike.wix.com/porto; 2nd fl, Largo de São Domingos 13; bike hire per 1/24hr €2.50/15; 10am-8pm)

Instituto dos Vinhos do Douro e do Porto WINE

14 MAP P42, B4

When area vintners apply for the certification that ultimately christens their casks with the term 'port', they bring vials to the labs just uphill from the river. The labs are off-limits to visitors, but you're welcome to explore the lobby exhibits, and the attached wine shop offers DIY tastings: from €1.50 to €6.50, ask for a card as you enter. (www.ivdp.pt; Rua Ferreira Borges 27; 11am-7pm Mon-Fri)

Porto Tours TOURS

15 MAP P42, E3

This excellent municipal service provides details of all the recommended tour operators, from city walking tours, Douro cruises and jaunts by Segway, bike and scooter to private taxi tours or helicopter rides over the city. As well as providing impartial advice, Porto Tours will make bookings for you. (222 000 045; www.portotours.com; 10am-7pm)

Eating

Taberna do Largo PORTUGUESE €

16 MAP P42, B3

Lit by wine-bottle lights, this sweet grocery store, deli and tavern is run with passion by Joana and Sofia. Tour Portugal with your taste buds with their superb array of hand-picked wines, which go brilliantly with tasting platters of smoked tuna, Alentejo *salpicão* sausage,

Azores São Jorge cheese, Beira *morcela* (blood sausage), *tremoços* (lupin beans) and more. (📞222 082 154; Largo de São Domingos 69; petiscos €2-14; ⏰5pm-midnight Tue-Thu, to 1am Fri, noon-1am Sat, noon-midnight Sun; 🛜)

Mercearia das Flores   DELI €

17 ❌ MAP P42, D2

This rustic-chic delicatessen/food store serves all-day *petiscos* made with organic regional products on the three tables and two counters of its bright and airy interior. You can also order wines by the glass, tea from the Azores and locally brewed Sovina beer. Try the spicy sardines and salad on dark, sweet *broa* cornbread. (Rua das Flores 110; petiscos €2.50-8.50; ⏰10.30am-9pm Mon-Sat, noon-8pm Sun; 🛜)

Chocolataria das Flores   CAFE €

18 ❌ MAP P42, D2

This enticingly cosy hole-in-the-wall cafe rustles up light bites such as quiches and salads, but really they are just the prelude to the main act: dessert. Come for the homemade chocolates, cakes, tarts, cookies, and hot chocolate so thick you can stand a spoon in it. Brunch will set you back a modest €10. (Rua das Flores 121; coffee & cake €2.50, snacks €4-7; ⏰10am-8pm)

Da Terra   VEGETARIAN €

19 ❌ MAP P42, D2

Porto's shift towards lighter, super-healthy food is reflected in the buffet served at Da Terra. This popular, contemporary bistro puts its own spin on vegetarian and vegan food

Mercearia das Flores

PAUL ABBITT RML / ALAMY STOCK PHOTO ©

Hammer Time: Porto's Mad Midsummer Party

Porto pulls out the stops, the bunting and the plastic hammers for one of Europe's wildest street parties – the **Festa de São João** (St John's Festival; ⏰ 24 Jun), celebrated in riotous style on 23 and 24 June. If ever the full force of love is going to hit you when you least expect it, it will be here – one of the festival's unique traditions is to thwack whoever you fancy over the head with a squeaky plastic hammer (*martelo*). For a more subtle approach, there are *manjericos* (potted basil plants with poems).

As you might expect, these head-spinning attacks cause much flirtatious giggling, squealing and chasing in the maze of narrow medieval lanes spilling down to the riverfront. The origins of the *festa* are apparently rooted in pagan rituals to celebrate the summer solstice and bountiful harvests. 'Bountiful' certainly sums up the city's streets on 23 June, as they teem with hammer-wielding locals scoffing grilled sardines, drinking *vinho*, dancing like there's no tomorrow and sending Chinese lanterns drifting into the night sky.

– from creative salads to Thai-style veggies and tagines. It also does a fine line in fresh-pressed juices and desserts. The website posts details of upcoming workshops and cookery courses. (📞 223 199 257; www. daterra.pt; Rua Mouzinho da Silveira 249; buffet €9.90; ⏰ noon-11pm;)

Mercador Café
CAFE €

20 ❌ MAP P42, D1

Mercador is a cute and cosy pit stop smack bang in the middle of one of Porto's prettiest streets, Rua das Flores. Browse the sweets cabinet for homemade cakes and pastries, settle for a simple toastie or order a traditional cooked lunch from the daily menu. (📞 223 323 041; www. facebook.com/mercadorcafe; Rua das Flores 180; snacks €3-6; ⏰ 9am-8pm Mon-Sat; 📶)

Café do Comércio
CAFE €

21 ❌ MAP P42, A4

Slip down a side street away from the crowds and you'll find this cute cubbyhole of a cafe, with quirky leaf etchings on the wall and just a handful of modern bistro-style tables. The menu is sweet 'n' simple, with excellent breakfasts (try the homemade muesli), great cakes and coffee, pancakes, toasties and always a vegan option or two. (📞 220 990 366; Rua do Comércio do Porto 124; snacks €2-6; ⏰ 9am-5pm Tue-Sat, to 1pm Sun; 🍴)

Cantina 32
PORTUGUESE €€

22 ❌ MAP P42, C2

Industrial-chic meets boho at this delightfully laid-back haunt, with its walls of polished concrete, mismatched crockery, verdant plants, and vintage knick-knacks ranging from a bicycle to an old typewriter. The menu is just as informal – *petiscos* such as *pica-pau* steak (bite-sized pieces of steak in a garlic-white-wine sauce), quail egg croquettes, and cheesecake served in a flower pot reveal a pinch of creativity. (📞222 039 069; www.cantina32.com; Rua das Flores 32; petiscos €3.50-20; ⏱12.30-3pm & 6.30-10.30pm Mon-Sat; 📶)

Puro 4050   MEDITERRANEAN €€

23 ⊗ MAP P42, B3

This chic Mediterranean-style restaurant and mozzarella bar is located in Porto's swanky dining precinct, and as a high ranker in the popularity stakes it usually requires prebooking. Bring your buddies along, as the menu is perfect for sharing. (📞222 011 852; www.puro4050.com; Largo de São Domingos 84; share plates €11-13, mains €11-25; ⏱12.30-3pm & 6.30-10.30pm Mon-Thu, to 11pm Fri & Sat)

Taberna dos Mercadores   PORTUGUESE €€

24 ⊗ MAP P42, D5

The chefs run a tight ship in the open kitchen at this curvaceous, softly lit, bottle-lined tavern, sizzling, stirring and delivering superb Portuguese grub with a smile from noon to night. On the menu are spot-on dishes as simple as *polvo com arroz no forno* (octopus rice baked in the oven), *feijoada*

(black bean one-pot), grilled fish and meats. (📞222 010 510; Rua dos Mercadores 36; mains €14-22; ⏱12.30-3.30pm & 7-11pm Tue-Sun)

Jimão   TAPAS €€

25 ⊗ MAP P42, D5

Many of the restaurants on Praça da Ribeira (p45) are tourist central, Jimão being the exception. Service is genuinely friendly, the upstairs dining room has a cracking view of Ribeira, and the tapas – garlicky *gambas* (prawns), codfish and octopus salad, sardine toasts and the like – are prepared with care and served with great wines. (📞220 924 660; www.jimao.pt; Praça da Ribeira 11; tapas €4-7; ⏱noon-10pm Wed-Mon)

Cantinho do Avillez   GASTRONOMY €€

26 ⊗ MAP P42, D3

Rock star chef José Avillez' latest venture is a welcome fixture on Porto's gastro scene. A bright, contemporary bistro with a retro spin, Cantinho keeps the mood casual and buzzy. On the menu are seasonal Portuguese dishes with a dash of imagination: from flaked *bacalhau* (dried salt-cod) with melt-in-the-mouth 'exploding' olives to giant red shrimps from the Algarve with Thai spices. (📞223 227 879; www.cantinhodoavillez.pt; Rua Mouzinho da Silveira 166; mains €18-40; ⏱12.30-3pm & 7pm-midnight Mon-Fri, 12.30pm-midnight Sat & Sun)

Bacalhau
PORTUGUESE €€

27 🍴 MAP P42, A6

The name *bacalhau* (dried salt-cod) should give you an inkling as to the star of the menu here. Snag a table on the walls to gaze at the river while digging into all-Portuguese *petiscos* and *bacalhau*-inspired dishes, be it fresh cod with an egg-yolk and cod roe *açorda* (stew) or codfish with turnip greens and chorizo. (🖉 222 010 521, 960 378 883; www.bacalhauporto.com; Muro dos Bacalhoeiros 153; petiscos €4.50-8.50, mains €12-16; ⏰ 11am-11pm Sun-Thu, to midnight Fri & Sat; 👬)

A Grade
PORTUGUESE €€

28 🍴 MAP P42, B6

Both a humble mum-and-dad operation and a masterwork of traditional fare, with generously portioned standouts such as baked octopus in butter and wine, braised pork cheeks and grilled seafood casseroles. Reservations recommended. (🖉 223 321 130; Rua de São Nicolau 9; mains €10-15; ⏰ 10.30am-midnight Mon-Sat; 🖉)

Traça
PORTUGUESE €€

29 🍴 MAP P42, C3

Happening Traça is tucked in a 17th-century building that once housed a pharmacy. Its retro-cool interior has nods to its rustic Portuguese roots in the form of *azulejos,* wood panelling and mounted stag antlers. It's big on soul food, with particularly outstanding meaty picks: T-bone steaks, slow-roast kid goat, confit of veal shank with vodka and the like.

Terrace seats are gold dust when it's sunny. (🖉 222 081 065; www.restaurantetraca.com; Largo de São Domingos 88; lunch menu €8.50, mains €14.50-36; ⏰ noon-3.30pm & 7pm-midnight Sun-Thu, to 2am Fri, 12.30-4.30pm & 7pm-2am Sat)

DOP
GASTRONOMY €€€

30 🍴 MAP P42, B3

Housed in a grand edifice, DOP is one of Porto's most stylish addresses, with its high ceilings and slick, monochrome interior. Much-feted chef Rui Paula puts a creative, seasonal twist on outstanding ingredients, with dish after delicate, flavour-packed dish skipping from octopus carpaccio to cod with lobster rice. The three-course lunch is terrific value at €27. (🖉 222 014 313; www.ruipaula.com; Largo de São Domingos 18; menus €27-90; ⏰ 7.30-11pm Mon, 12.30-3pm & 7.30-11pm Tue-Sat; 🛜)

LSD
MODERN EUROPEAN €€€

31 🍴 MAP P42, C3

Nothing to do with mind-bending drugs, this slick, contemporary bistro sets the scene with soft lighting and lemon and grey hues. The chef cooks clean, bright flavours with a unique touch, be it free-range chicken served with nectarines or watermelon ice cream with penny-royal ice cream. There's always a good buzz. (🖉 223 231 268, 910 298 589; www.facebook.com/largodesao-domingos; Largo de São Domingos 78; lunch special/menu €9/10.50, mains €18-20; ⏰ 9am-2am; 🛜 👬)

Ode Porto Wine House
PORTUGUESE €€€

32 MAP P42, C6

A slow-food hideaway just up from the Douro, with chestnut-wood beams, exposed stone walls, and slate tables on wine barrels. The ingredients are all Portuguese – bread from Bragança, oregano from the Algarve, smoked pork from Minho and sheep's cheese from Alentejo – and the dishes have a story. Reservations required. (☏ 913 200 010; www.facebook.com/odeportowinehouse; Largo do Terreiro 7; mains €26-32, menus €65-95; ⊙ 7-10.30pm Tue-Sun)

Drinking

Prova
WINE BAR

33 MAP P42, B4

Diogo, the passionate owner, explains the finer nuances of Portuguese wine at this chic, stone-walled bar, where relaxed jazz plays. Stop by for a two-glass tasting (€5), or sample wines by the glass – including beefy Douros, full-bodied Dãos and crisp Alentejo whites. These marry well with sharing plates (€14) of local hams and cheeses. Diogo's port tonics are legendary. (www.prova.com.pt; Rua Ferreira Borges 86; ⊙ 5pm-1am; 🛜)

Wine Quay Bar
WINE BAR

34 MAP P42, C6

Sunset is prime-time viewing on the terrace of this terrific wine bar by the Rio Douro. As you gaze across to the graceful arc of the Ponte Dom Luís I and over to the port cellars of Vila Nova de Gaia, you can sample some cracking Portuguese wines and appetisers, such as cured ham, cheese, olives and the like. (www.winequaybar.com; Cais da Estiva 111; ⊙ 4-11pm Mon-Sat; 🛜)

Portologia
WINE BAR

35 MAP P42, D5

This cosy wine bar is an excellent place to sample the fine quaffs of Porto, with over 200 different ports on offer. If you fall in love with a certain wine, you can usually buy a whole bottle (or even send a case home). Three-port tastings start at €10. (www.vinologia.pt; Rua de São João 28-30; ⊙ 11am-midnight)

Wine Box
WINE BAR

36 MAP P42, D4

Wine crates turn the interior into quite a feature at this uber-hip, black-walled wine bar, with a good buzz and some 450 (at the last count) wines on the menu, some of which are available by the glass. *Petiscos* pair nicely with these. Service teeters on the indifferent, however, and the newfangled tablet menu can be hard to get the hang of. (www.thewineboxporto.com; Rua dos Mercadores 72; ⊙ 1.30pm-midnight Thu-Tue; 🛜)

Entertainment

Casa da Mariquinhas
FADO

37 MAP P42, D3

Follow the strains of fado to this traditional, highly atmospheric

Wine Tasting Porto-Style

Housed in the grand Palácio da Bolsa, the ViniPortugal (p39) tasting room is the perfect way to brush up on your knowledge of Portuguese wines (including those produced in the nearby Douro). An 'enocard' costing €3 is your ticket to tasting two to four wines from a selection of 12 chosen from different regions of the country. The friendly, clued-up staff will talk you through them.

tavern, with live fado at 9pm from Wednesday to Saturday. There is a minimum consumption of €37 per person. Advance bookings recommended. (www.casadamariquinhas.pt; Rua de São Sebastião 25; ⏰8pm-1am Wed & Thu, to 2am Fri & Sat)

Hot Five Jazz & Blues Club   JAZZ

38 ⭐ MAP P42, H4

True to its name, this spot hosts live jazz and blues as well as the occasional acoustic, folk or all-out jam session. It's a modern but intimate space, with seating at small round tables, both fronting the stage and on an upper balcony. Concerts often start later than scheduled. (📞934 328 583; www.hotfive.pt; Largo Actor Dias 51; ⏰10pm-3am Wed-Sun)

Shopping

Oliva & Co   FOOD

39 🅰 MAP P42, B4

Everything you ever wanted to know about Portuguese olive oil becomes clear at this store, which maps out the country's six Protected Designation of Origin (PDO) regions produc-

ing the extra-virgin stuff. Besides superb oils and olives, you'll find biscuits, chocolate and soaps made with olive oil. Try before you buy or join one of the in-depth tastings. (www.olivaeco.com; Rua Ferreira Borges 60; ⏰10am-7pm Mon-Fri, to 8pm Sat)

Zinda Atelier   CERAMICS

40 🅰 MAP P42, B4

Porto-based ceramic artist Adosinda Pereira can often be seen making her latest creation at her little studio in the heart of Ribeira. If you're in the market for a lovingly handmade *andorinha* (swallow) or intricate *azulejo*, this is the go-to place. (http://zindaatelier.com; Rua Ferreira Borges 63; ⏰2.30-7.30pm Mon-Sat)

Loja das Conservas   FOOD

41 🅰 MAP P42, D2

An ode to the humble tinned fish, this store is stacked to the rafters with bold, retro-wrapped cans of tuna, *bacalhau* and sardines plain and spicy. It stocks popular brands such as Santa Catarina and Viana Pesca, which at between €2.50 and €4 a pop make funky gifts. Look out for the stuffed sardine as you enter. (Rua de Mouzinho da Silveira 240; ⏱10.30am-8pm Mon-Sat)

Claus Porto
COSMETICS

42 🔒 MAP P42, C3

Beautifully packaged Claus Porto luxury soaps, fragrances, creams, colognes and candles fill the shelves of latest store in the city where the venerable brand was born in 1887. The hand-crafted products draw on traditional Portuguese ingredients and are illustrated with vintage graphic designs. (https://clausporto.com; Rua das Flores 22; ⏱10am-8pm)

43 Branco
ARTS & CRAFTS

43 🔒 MAP P42, C2

One-of-a-kind Portuguese crafts, fashion and interior design take centre stage at this new concept store, which brings a breath of fresh creativity to Rua das Flores. Here you'll find everything from filigree, gem-studded Maria Branco jewellery to funky sardine pencil cases, Porto-inspired Lubo T-shirts and beautifully packaged Bonjardim soaps. (Rua das Flores 43; ⏱11am-7pm Mon-Sat)

Chocolateria Ecuador
CHOCOLATE

44 🔒 MAP P42, E1

If chocolate is the elixir of the gods, this place is surely heaven on earth. Nip in to find a retro-cool wonderland of beautifully packaged Portuguese chocolate bars, truffles – including a deliciously dark number with port wine – pralines, macaroons and bonbons. They

make perfect edible gifts. (www.chocolatariaequador.com; Rua das Flores 298; ⏱11am-7.30pm)

Retrosaria das Flores
ARTS & CRAFTS

45 🔒 MAP P42, D2

This retro-flavoured haberdashery is a wonderful place to browse for buttons, wool, embroidery and flamboyantly printed fabrics (some of which have been fashioned into eye-catching bags). It also arranges workshops in oft-forgotten handicrafts such as felting and crocheting. (Rua das Flores 104; ⏱9.30am-1pm & 2-7pm Mon-Sat)

Tradições
GIFTS & SOUVENIRS

46 🔒 MAP P42, E1

For Portuguese souvenirs, Tradições is the real deal. In this sweet, friendly shop, the owner knows the story behind every item – from bags beautifully fashioned from Alentejo cork to Algarvian *flôr de sal* (hand-harvested sea salt), Lousã honey to Lazuli *azulejos*. (Rua das Flores 238; ⏱10am-7pm)

Loja das Tábuas
ARTS & CRAFTS

47 🔒 MAP P42, B3

As the name suggests, this shop specialises in quality Portuguese oak *tábuas* (chopping boards) in all shapes and sizes (starting at around €16), as well as cork products and chunky wooden toys. We particularly like the cork sardine wall hangings. (www.lojadastabuas.pt; Largo de São Domingos 20; ⏱11am-8pm)

Explore ✦

Aliados & Bolhão

This vibrant neighbourhood hides boutiques, old-school grocery stores, pavement cafes, and baroque churches dazzling with azulejos (hand-painted tiles) down its backstreets. This is where Porto comes to market-shop, eat and play, with the Galerias enticing partygoers to its speakeasy-style bars, slinky cocktail-sipping lounges and live-music venues after dark.

Rewind to an age of lace-gloved farewells at beautifully tiled São Bento Train Station (p60), then continue your walk on beaux arts boulevard Avenida dos Aliados (p60). Nearby Rua de Santa Catarina is made for strolling — begin at Capela das Almas (p60) and end at sumptuous (if touristy) Café Majestic (p68). Further west, climb baroque Torre dos Clérigos (p60) for cracking city views, before popping across to neo-Gothic bookstore Livraria Lello (p60). Revive over éclairs at Leitaria da Quinta do Paço (p65), then check out twin baroque churches Igreja do Carmo (p88) and Igreja das Carmelitas (p88).

Book a table for dinner at delightfully mellow Flor dos Congregados (p63) or gourmet Euskalduna Studio (p65).

Getting There & Around

Ⓜ **Metro** Stops include Trindade, Aliados and São Bento.

🚋 **Tram** Tram 18 links Jardim da Cordoaria to the Massarelos district. Line 22 makes a loop of the centre between Carmo and Batalha/Funicular dos Guindais.

🚌 **Bus** A number of bus lines converge at the southern end of Avenida dos Aliados and Cordoaria.

Aliados & Bolhão Map on p58

Town hall, Avenida dos Aliados (p60) TRABANTOS / SHUTTERSTOCK ©

Walking Tour 🥾

Aliados & Bolhão

Allow at least half a day for this walk from Porto's monumental Avenida dos Aliados boulevard to the haunting sculptures of Spanish sculptor Juan Muñoz in Jardim da Cordoaria. En route you'll take in the banter of one of the city's best old-school grocery stores, exquisite baroque and Gothic churches, a tower with a view and the magical bookshop that continues to put the Harry Potter in Porto.

Walk Facts

Start Avenida dos Aliados
End Jardim da Cordoaria
Length 3km; 3½ hours

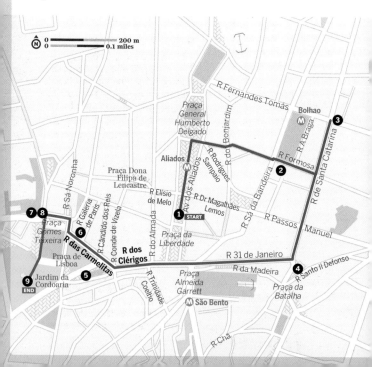

❶ Avenida dos Aliados

Paris has the Champs Élysées and Porto has the **Avenida dos Aliados** (p60), a stately boulevard built high and mighty from pale marble and granite, with all the beaux arts trimmings. Its centrepiece, *câmara municipal* (town hall), is topped by a 70m tower.

❷ A Pérola do Bolhão

Turn right onto Rua Formosa and you'll be struck by one of Porto's most ornate art nouveau shop facades at **A Pérola do Bolhão** (p72). The old-school deli opened its doors in 1917 and now brims with Portuguese cheeses and charcuterie, olives, nuts, dried fruit and wine.

❸ Capela das Almas

On the pedestrian-only Rua de Santa Catarina, thronged with shoppers, your gaze will be drawn to the 18th-century **Capela das Almas** (p60), with blue and white *azulejo* friezes dancing flamboyantly across its facade.

❹ Praça da Batalha

Wander south to **Praça da Batalha**, a grand plaza home to the splendidly tiled baroque Igreja de Santo Ildefonso (p61). Across the way the Teatro Nacional São João (p71), the spitting image of Paris' Palais Garnier in miniature, demands attention.

❺ Torre dos Clérigos

Amble along Rua de 31 Janeiro and continue along Praça da Liberdade, dominated by an equestrian statue of a dashing King Pedro IV. You'll emerge at Nicolau Nasoni's baroque **tower** (p60). Ascend the 225-step spiral staircase for fabulous city views.

❻ Livraria Lello

Cross Praça de Lisboa and you can't miss this fanciful 1906 neo-Gothic **bookshop** (p60) at the foot of the bar-lined Galeria district. Its bewitching interior with stained-glass skylight and twisting staircase inspired JK Rowling's Harry Potter books during her stint living in Porto.

❼ Igreja do Carmo

It's just a two-minute toddle from here to the rococo **Igreja do Carmo** (p88), one side of which is clad top to toe in stunning *azulejos* that depict the founding of the Carmelite order.

❽ Igreja das Carmelitas

Sidling up to Igreja do Carmo, the 17th-century **Igreja das Carmelitas** (p88) is modest on the outside and staggeringly ornate on the inside. The twin churches are separated by a 1m-wide house, once the dividing line between the monks of Carmo and the Carmelite nuns.

❾ Jardim da Cordoaria

Round out your walk at the central **Jardim da Cordoaria** (p89), where trams rumble on past. With its ponds, sculpture-dotted gardens and tree shade, it's a relaxed spot for a breather.

CEDOFEITA

1

R Mirante

2

R Mártires da Liberdade

R da Conceição

R Dr Ricardo Jorge

R do Almada

🔒 54   11 ⊚
Fold 'n' Visit

City Centre Turismo ℹ️

R Clube dos Fenianos

Tourist Police

Praça General Humberto Delgado

Tv de Cedofeita

🔒 47   ✕ 25   ✕ 20   ⊚ 37

R da Picaria

18
⊚ Workshops Pop Up
8 ⊚

R Ramalho Ortigão

ALIADOS

Aliados Ⓜ

Tv do Carregal

R de Cedofeita

R José Falcão

3

✕ 21
Praça Carlos Alberto

⊚ 24

Zenith Brunch & Cocktails

R Sá Noronha

⊚ 31

R Ceuta

Sincelo

Praça Dona Filipa de Lencastre

Av dos Aliados

⊚ 2
Avenida dos Aliados

R Dr

⊚ 30
Leitaria da Quinta do Paço ●

⊚ 28
O Diplomata

R Sta Teresa

17
✕ 51 🔒
R Fábrica
22 ✕

4

Praça Gomes Fernandes
32 ⊚

R Galeria de Paris

R Cândido dos Reis

R Conde de Vizela

49 🔒

56 🔒

R do Almada

R Sampaio

Praça Gomes Teixeira
Livraria Lello 3
⊚ 38   ✕ 26 ⊚ 35
⊚ 39
✕ 29 ⊚ 40
🔒 57

Praça da Liberdade

Praça Parada Leitão

Tv do Carmo

R das Carmelitas

52 ⊚
Praça de Lisboa
34 ⊚   ⊚ 41

Igreja dos Clérigos
6

R dos Clérigos

Porto Walkers

⊚ 9

Praça Almeida Garrett

5

Jardim da Cordoaria

⊚ 4
Torre dos Clérigos

15 ✕

R dos Caldeireiros

R Trindade Coelho

São Bento Ⓜ

MIRAGAIA

R São Bento da Vitória

R da Vitória

R das Flores

R Mouzinho da Silveira

Av Dom Afonso Henriques

6

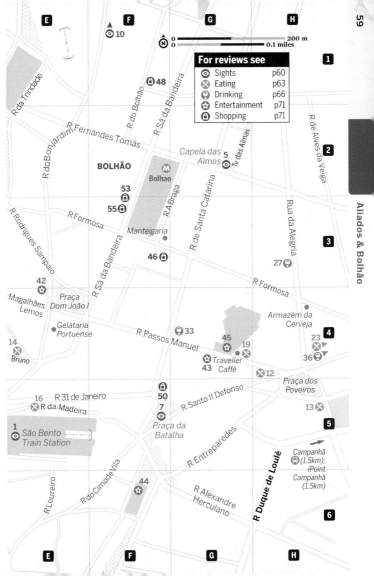

E F G H

For reviews see

⊙	Sights	p60
⊗	Eating	p63
🍷	Drinking	p66
❂	Entertainment	p71
🔒	Shopping	p71

N 0 — 200 m
0 — 0.1 miles

⊙ 10

🔒 48

R da Trindade
R do Bolhão
R Sá da Bandeira
R de Alves da Veiga

R Fernandes Tomás
R do Bonjardim

BOLHÃO

Capela das Almas
5 ⊙ Tv das Almas

Ⓜ Bolhao

53 🔒
55 🔒

R Formosa
R Sá da Bandeira
R A Braga
R de Santa Catarina

Manteigaria 🍷

46 🔒

Rua da Alegria

27 🍷

R Formosa

R Rodrigues Sampaio

42 ❂
Praça Dom João I
Magalhães Lemos

Gelataria Portuense

R Passos Manuel

33 ⊗

45 ❂
19 ⊗

Armazém da Cerveja

23 ⊗
36 🍷

14 ❂
Bruno

43 ❂ Traveller Caffé

12 ⊗

Praça dos Poveiros

13 ⊗

16 ❂
R 31 de Janeiro
R da Madeira

50 🔒
7 ⊙

R Santo Il Defonso

1 ⊙ São Bento Train Station

Praça da Batalha

R Entreparedes

Campanhã 🚉 (1.5km); iPoint Campanhã (1.5km)

R Loureiro
R do Cimo de Vila

44 ❂

R Alexandre Herculano

R Duque de Loulé

E F G H

Sights

São Bento Train Station
HISTORIC BUILDING

1 ⊙ MAP P58, E5

One of the world's most beautiful train stations, beaux arts São Bento wings you back to a more graceful age of rail travel. Completed in 1903, it seems to have been imported from 19th-century Paris with its mansard roof. But the dramatic *azulejo* panels of historic scenes in the front hall are the real attraction. Designed by Jorge Colaço in 1930, some 20,000 tiles depict historic battles (including Henry the Navigator's conquest of Ceuta), as well as the history of transport. (Praça Almeida Garrett; ⊘5am-1am)

Avenida dos Aliados
AREA

2 ⊙ MAP P58, D4

Lined with bulging, beaux arts facades and capped by the stately câmara municipal (municipal council), this avenida recalls grand Parisian imitators such as Buenos Aires and Budapest. The avenue's central plaza was restored a few years back and often hosts pop-up book, comic and art festivals and exhibitions.

Livraria Lello
HISTORIC BUILDING

3 ⊙ MAP P58, B4

Ostensibly a bookshop, but even if you're not after books, don't miss this exquisite 1906 neo-Gothic confection, with its lavishly carved plaster resembling wood and a stained-glass skylight. Feels magical? Its intricately wrought, curiously twisting staircase was supposedly the inspiration for the one in the Harry Potter books, which JK Rowling partly wrote in Porto while working here as an English teacher from 1991 to 1993. (www.livrarialello.pt; Rua das Carmelitas 144; admission €5; ⊘10am-7.30pm Mon-Fri, 10am-7pm Sat, 11am-7pm Sun; ♿)

Torre dos Clérigos
TOWER

4 ⊙ MAP P58, B5

Sticking out on Porto's skyline like a sore thumb – albeit a beautiful baroque one – this 76m-high tower was designed by Italian-born master Nicolau Nasoni in the mid-1700s. Climb its 225-step spiral staircase for phenomenal views over Porto's tiled rooftops, spires and the curve of the Douro to the port-wine lodges in Gaia. It also harbours an exhibition that chronicles the history of the tower's architects and residents. (www.torredosclerigos.pt; Rua de São Filipe de Nery; admission €5; ⊘9am-7pm)

Capela das Almas
CHURCH

5 ⊙ MAP P58, G2

On Rua de Santa Catarina stands the strikingly ornate, *azulejo*-clad Capela das Almas. Magnificent blue-and-white panels here depict scenes from the lives of various saints, including the death of St Francis and the martyrdom of St Catherine. Interestingly, Eduardo Leite painted the tiles in a classic 18th-century style, though they actually date back to the early 20th century. (Rua de Santa Catarina 428; ⏱7.30am-7pm Mon-Fri, 7.30am-1pm & 6-7pm Sat)

Igreja dos Clérigos CHURCH

6 ◉ MAP P58, C5

Nicolau Nasoni designed the Igreja dos Clérigos, with its theatrical facade and unusual, oval-shaped nave, resembling a Fabergé egg due to its dusky pink marble walls, profusion of cherubs and gilded wedding cake of an altar. (Rua dos Clérigos; admission free; ⏱9am-7pm)

Praça da Batalha SQUARE

7 ◉ MAP P58, F5

At the southern end of Rua de Santa Catarina is the lovely, eclectic Praça da Batalha, framed by Nasoni's gracefully baroque **Igreja de Santo Ildefonso** (⏱3-6.30pm Mon,

9am-noon & 3-6.30pm Tue-Sun) with its twin bell towers, and the lavishly romantic Teatro Nacional São João (p71), built in the style of Paris' Palais Garnier.

Workshops Pop Up COOKING

8 ◉ MAP P58, C3

This cool indie arts, crafts and interior design store hosts regular three-hour, hands-on cookery workshops, followed by lunch or dinner with wine pairing. Themes range from healthy snacks and Indian food to Cook and Taste Portugal, where you'll learn to cook Portuguese classics like *bacalhau à lagareiro* (codfish cooked in extra virgin olive oil) and *pastéis de nata* (Portuguese-style custard tarts). (☎966 974 119; www.workshops-popup.com; Rua do Almada 275; 3hr class incl lunch or dinner €35)

São Bento Train Station (p60)

BENNY MARTY / SHUTTERSTOCK ©

On the Tiles in Porto

One of the delights of taking a wander through the narrow streets of Porto is the *azulejos* (hand-painted tiles) you will encounter. Old and new, utilitarian and decorative, plain and geometrically patterned, they dance across the facades of houses, the walls of cafes and bars, the tunnels of metro stations and the opulent interiors of churches.

One of the largest and most exquisite panels of *azulejos* covers the Igreja do Carmo (p88). Silvestre Silvestri's 1912 magnum opus illustrates the founding of the Carmelite order.

Stroll along pedestrianised Rua de Santa Catarina for a feast of *azulejos* at the Capela das Almas (p60), where a frieze by Eduardo Leite recounts the lives of various saints.

São Bento (p60) is a veritable ode to *azulejo* art. Spelling out momentous events in Portuguese history, including the Battle of Valdevez (1140), the arrival of King João I and Philippa of Lancaster in Porto (1387) and the Conquest of Ceuta (1415), the friezes designed by master Jorge Colaço in 1930 are so vivid and detailed you can almost hear the fanfare and the stampeding cavalry.

Porto Walkers
WALKING

9 MAP P58, D5

Peppered with anecdotes and personality, these young, fun, three-hour guided walking tours are a great intro to Porto, starting at 10.45am daily. The tours are free (well, the guides work for tips, so give what you can). Simply turn up at the meeting point on Praça da Liberdade and look out for the guide in the red T-shirt. (📞918 291 519; www.portowalkers.pt; Praça da Liberdade, Avenida dos Aliados)

Tuk Tour
TOURS

10 MAP P58, F1

Tuk-tuks are maybe more Thailand than Porto, but these electric numbers are an eco-cool way to buzz around the city as your clued-up guide shares anecdotes. Tours skip from two-hour spins from Gaia to Foz (€25) to 1½-hour night tours of the illuminated city (€25). Tours either depart from Rua das Carmelitas or Avenida Ramos Pinto. (📞915 094 443; www.tuktourporto.com; Rua do Bonjardim 905)

Fold 'n' Visit
CYCLING

11 MAP P58, D1

Close to Trindade metro station, Fold 'n' Visit offers bike rentals and upbeat city tours. A three-hour spin of Porto downtown costs €17 to €25 per person, depending on group numbers. (📞220 997 106; www.topbiketoursportugal.com; Rua Alferes Malheiro 139; rental per half-/full day from €13/17)

Eating

Cafe Santiago
PORTUGUESE €

12 MAP P58, H4

This is hands down one of the best places to try Porto's classic gut-busting treat, the *francesinha* – a thick, open-faced sandwich piled with cheese, sausage, egg and/or assorted meats, plus a tasty, rich beer sauce. This classic will set you back €9.75, which might seem pricey for a sandwich, but trust us: it's a meal in itself. (222 055 797; http://caferestaurantesantiago.com.pt; Rua Passos Manuel 226; mains €8-12; noon-11pm Mon-Sat)

Casa Guedes
PORTUGUESE €

13 MAP P58, H5

A roast-pork sandwich may seem simple on paper, but here it's a thing of beauty – tasty, filling, a bargain at €2.90 and served all day. Space is tight at this no-frills *tasca* (tavern), so be prepared to wait for a table inside or on the little terrace on the square. (Praça dos Poveiros 130; mains €6-9; 8.30am-10pm Mon-Sat)

Flor dos Congregados
PORTUGUESE €€

14 MAP P58, E4

Tucked away down a narrow alley, this softly lit, family-run restaurant brims with stone-walled, wood-beamed, art-slung nooks. The frequently changing blackboard menu goes with the seasons. (222 002 822; www.flordoscongregados.pt; Travessa dos Congregados 11; mains €8-16; 7-10pm Mon-Wed, noon-3pm & 7-11pm Thu-Sat)

All In Porto
PORTUGUESE €€

15 MAP P58, C5

Wine-barrel tables, lanterns and funky Porto murals create a hip, laid-back space for sampling a stellar selection of Portuguese wines and nicely prepared *petiscos* (tapas). These range from flame-grilled *chouriço* (spicy sausage) to spicy sardine roe, cheeses and *conservas* (canned fish). Quiet enough for conversing, it's also a chilled spot to begin or end an evening over drinks. (220 993 829; www.facebook.com/allinporto; Rua Arquitecto Nicolau Nasoni 17; petiscos €8-22, tasting boards €12-16; 10am-midnight Mon-Fri, noon-midnight Sat & Sun)

Tapabento
TAPAS €€

16 MAP P58, E5

There's a good buzz at split-level Tapabento, discreetly tucked behind São Bento train station. Stone walls, bright prints and cheek-by-jowl tables set the scene for outstanding tapas and Douro wines. Sharing is the way to go – be it fresh oysters with shallot vinaigrette, razor clams with garlic and coriander or Azores cheese with rocket and walnuts. (912 881 272, 222 034 115; www.tapabento.com; Rua da Madeira 222; tapas & sharing plates €3-20, mains €14-22; 7-11pm Tue, noon-11pm Wed & Thu, to midnight Fri & Sat, noon-5pm & 7-10.30pm Sun)

Tascö
PORTUGUESE €€

17 ✖ MAP P58, C4

Tascö's slick, banquette-lined interior is playfully peppered with personality in the form of a tree-shaped bookcase and a huge blackboard for scrawling messages. Super-friendly staff keep the good vibes and *petiscos* coming – lip-smacking little dishes of *rojões* (pork cooked in garlic, wine and cumin), *morcela* (black pudding), octopus and the like, paired with craft beers, wines and ports. (☎919 803 323, 222 010 763; www.facebook.com/pg/soldout arena; Rua do Almada 151A; petiscos €4.50-12.50; ⏱noon-1am)

Cruel
FUSION €€

18 ✖ MAP P58, C2

How cruel are you? This is what you'll be asked at this on-trend restaurant, where the menu is graded according to how adventurous your appetite is: 'fearful', 'cautious' or 'cruel'. The look is slick and urban, and the menu has inventive riffs on classics – think 'hallucinating mushroom risotto' and 'electric carpaccio' – many of which are big enough to share. (☎924 400 259; www.cruel.pt; Rua da Picaria 86; mains €13-25, petiscos €4-6; ⏱7.30-11.30pm Mon, Tue & Thu, 12.30-2.30pm & 7.30pm-1am Fri, 1-3pm & 7.30pm-1am Sat, 1-3pm & 7.30-11pm Sun)

Tripeiro
PORTUGUESE €€

19 ✖ MAP P58, G4

As fads come and go, restaurants dishing up good old-fashioned Por-

tuguese grub are becoming scarce. Cue Tripeiro: a cosy, nouveau-rustic tavern where you can dig into the likes of *tripas à moda do Porto* (Porto-style tripe and white bean stew) and *bacalhau com broa* (codfish with cornbread crust). (☎222 038 075, 925 908 852; www.restaurante tripeiro.com; Rua de Passos Manuel 195; mains €10.50-16, 1-/2-/3-course lunch €7.50/8.50/10.50; ⏱12.30-3pm & 7-11pm Mon-Sat, 12.30-3pm Sun)

Flow
MEDITERRANEAN €€

20 ✖ MAP P58, B2

Huge wicker lamps cast flattering light onto the brick-walled dining room of this stylishly converted neo-Arabic building with high ceilings. On warm evenings retreat to the inner courtyard to sip cocktails before enjoying Med-inspired dishes such as citrus-spiked tuna ceviche, octopus confit with black polenta, and *osso bucco* (veal shanks) with saffron risotto. (☎222 054 016; www.flowrestaurant.pt; Rua da Conceição 63; mains €17-29; ⏱7.45pm-midnight Mon, 12.45-3pm & 7.45pm-midnight Tue-Sat)

Camafeu
MODERN PORTUGUESE €€

21 ✖ MAP P58, B3

Visiting Camafeu, which overlooks Praça Carlos Alberto, is like eating in a friend's stylish 1st-floor apartment. Dishes such as slow-cooked pork cheek with *alheira* (a light, garlicky sausage of poultry or game), hazelnut and mushroom crumble and green asparagus are prepared with love and served with flair.

Top Sweet Treats

Manteigaria (Map p58, F3; Rua de Alexandre Braga 24; pastel de nata €1; ⏰8am-10pm Mon-Fri, to 7pm Sat) For our money, this bakery rolls out the city's finest *pastéis de nata* (custard tarts), served oven-warm. You can watch the bakers do their thing in the kitchen.

Sincelo (Map p58, C3; www.gelatariasincelo.com; Rua de Ceuta 54; ice cream €2.50-5; ⏰1-10.30pm Tue-Thu & Sun, to 12.30am Fri & Sat) One of the best gelatarias in town to pick up a properly creamy, fruity ice-cream cone. Enough said.

Leitaria da Quinta do Paço (Map p58, B4; www.leitariadaquintadopaco. com; Praça Guilherme Gomes Fernandes 47; éclairs €1.40; ⏰9am-8pm Mon-Thu, to 9pm Fri & Sat) Since 1920 this cafe-patisserie has served feather-light éclairs in myriad flavours, from classic lemon to the more unusual blue cheese, apple and fennel.

Gelataria Portuense (Map p58, E4; www.gelatariaportuense.pt; Rua do Bonjardim 136; 1 scoop €2.20, 6 gelato tasting €9; ⏰12.30-7pm Sun-Thu, to 10pm Fri & Sat) Ana is the gelato queen at this parlour, with scoops from dark chocolate to port wine, Earl Grey and lime.

There's room for just a handful of lucky diners in the chandelier-lit salon, which boasts French windows, antique furnishings and a polished wooden floor. (☎937 493 557; www. facebook.com/camafeu83; Praça Carlos Alberto 83; mains €15-19; ⏰6.30-11pm Tue-Sat; ♿)

MUU STEAK €€€

 22 MAP P58, C4

So you came for the steak, right? Wise decision. A welcome newcomer to Porto's food scene, MUU has carved out a name for itself with outstanding cuts of beef. Homemade Scotch eggs and cheese gratins prelude the main act: a garlic-rubbed rib-eye, say, or tender Black Angus steak. Either

way, you won't leave hungry. (☎914 784 032; www.muusteakhouse.com; Rua do Almada 149A; mains €22-32; ⏰7pm-midnight Wed-Mon)

Euskalduna Studio GASTRONOMY €€€

23 MAP P58, H4

Everyone loves surprises, especially edible ones prepared with flawless execution, experimental finesse and a nod to the seasons. Just 16 lucky diners (eight at the green marble counter peeking into the kitchen, eight at oak tables) get to sample Vasco Coelho Santos' stunning 10-course menus that allow flavours and textures to shine. (☎935 335 301; www.euskaldunastudio.pt; Rua de Santo Ildefonso 404;

Get Along to Taste Porto

Loosen a belt notch for the superb downtown food tours offered by **Taste Porto** (📱920 503 302; www.tasteporto.com; downtown food tour adult/child €65/42, vintage food tour €70/42, photo food experience €49; ⏱downtown food tour 10.45am & 4pm Tue-Sat, vintage food tour 10am & 4.15pm Mon-Sat, photo food experience 9.45am daily), where you'll sample everything from Porto's best slow-roast-pork sandwich to éclairs, fine wines, cheese and coffee. Friendly, knowledgeable guide André and his team lead these indulgent and insightful 3½-hour walking tours, which take in viewpoints and historic back lanes en route to restaurants, grocery stores and cafes.

10-course tasting menu €80; ⏱7-10pm Wed-Sat)

Drinking

Aduela   BAR

27 MAP P58, B3

Retro and hip but not self-consciously so, chilled Aduela bathes in the nostalgic orange glow of its glass lights, which illuminate the green walls and mishmash of vintage furnishings. Once a sewing machine warehouse, today it's where friends gather to converse over wine and appetising *petiscos*

(€3 to €8). (Rua das Oliveiras 36; ⏱3pm-2am Mon, 10am-2am Tue-Thu, to 4am Fri & Sat, 3pm-midnight Sun)

Museu d'Avó   BAR

25 🚌 MAP P58, B2

The name translates as 'Grandmother's Museum' and indeed it's a gorgeous rambling attic of a bar, crammed with cabinets, old clocks, *azulejos* and gramophones, with curios hanging from its rafters. Lanterns and candles illuminate young *tripeiros* (Porto residents) locked in animated conversation as the house beats spin. If you get the late-night munchies, it also whips up tasty *petiscos* (€2 to €8). (Travessa de Cedofeita 54; ⏱8pm-4am Mon-Sat)

Era uma Vez em Paris   BAR

26 🚌 MAP P58, C4

A little flicker of bohemian Parisian flair in the heart of Porto, Era uma Vez em Paris time warps you back to the more decadent 1920s. Its ruby-red walls, retro furnishings and frilly lampshades spin a warm, intimate cocoon for coffee by day and drinks by night. DJs keep the mood mellow with indie rock and funk beats. (Rua Galeria de Paris 106; ⏱7pm-2am Mon-Wed, to 4am Thu-Sat, 9pm-2am Sun)

Letraria   CRAFT BEER

27 🚌 MAP P58, H3

Craft beer bars are springing up all over Porto, but Letraria is a standout for its uber-chilled beer garden. Around half of the 20 or so beers on tap are the creations of Portuguese brand Letra, while the remainder are predominantly sourced from other domestic producers. (☎939 348 069; www.facebook.com/letraria craftbeergardenporto; Rua da Alegria 101; ⏰5pm-midnight Mon, Wed & Thu, 5pm-2am Fri & Sat, 4-11pm Sun)

Bonaparte Downtown PUB

28 🚇 MAP P58, B4

Lanterns cast a warm glow across the cosy, knick-knack-crammed, wood-heavy interior at this pleasingly relaxed number, which morphs from a low-key spot to sip a predinner beer to a much livelier haunt later in the evening. (www.facebook.com/bonapartedowntown; Praça Guilherme Gomes Fernandes 40; ⏰5pm-2am Sun-Thu, to 3am Fri & Sat)

La Bohème WINE BAR

29 🚇 MAP P58, B4

With a high-ceilinged, Scandi-style pine interior, La Bohème is one of the most stylish, intimate bars on Rua Galeria de Paris. It's a nicely chilled choice for pairing fine wines with *petiscos*. DJs spin as the evening wears on. (www.laboheme.com.pt; Rua Galeria de Paris 40; ⏰6pm-2am Tue-Thu, 6pm-4am Fri & Sat, 7pm-2am Sun)

Moustache CAFE

30 🚇 MAP P58, B3

Ease into the day gently or wind it out over drinks and mellow beats at this urban-cool cafe with edge. The armchairs are perfect for dawdling over a robust coffee or smoothie

and snacks such as filled croissants and cakes. Products are mostly organic and fair trade, and it also has lactose-free options. (www.moustache.pt; Praça Carlos Alberto 104; ⏰10am-8pm Sun-Thu, to 2am Fri & Sat; 📶)

Baixa Bar COCKTAIL BAR

With its curving walls and mirrored room, this retro-chic bar is decadent and daring when it comes to its zesty craft cocktails, such as the palate-awakening house special with white port and passionfruit. As the night wears on, things crank up a notch with DJs and dancing. Located beside Plano B (see 40 🚇 Map p58, C4). (www.facebook.com/pg/baixa bar; Rua Cândido dos Reis 52; ⏰6pm-2am Sun-Thu, to 4am Fri & Sat)

Gulden Draak – BierHuis Porto PUB

31 🚇 MAP P58, B3

A long polished wooden bar, backlit walls lined with bottles, and intimate booths for quaffing and conversing await at this new Belgian-style beerhouse. Pull up a stool to sip Van Steenberge speciality beers, such as the namesake Gulden Draak Brewmaster, aged in single-malt whisky barrels. (Rua de José Falcão 82; ⏰4pm-midnight Mon-Wed, to 2am Fri & Sat)

Cervejaria do Carmo CRAFT BEER

32 🚇 MAP P58, A4

With around 100 types of beer sourced from Portuguese and international producers, you won't

Best Spots for Brunch

O Diplomata (Map p58, B3; ☎ 222 050 482; www.facebook.com/o diplomatabar; Rua de José Falcão 32; pancakes €5-10; ⊙10am-8pm Mon-Tue & Thu-Sat, to 4pm Sun) Pancake heaven, with sweet and savoury toppings, plus savoury salad, toasties, açaí bowls and fresh juices. Swing by for brunch (available until a leisurely 4pm). Can't decide? Check the blackboard wall for the pancake of the week.

Zenith (Map p58, B3; ☎ 220 171 557; www.facebook.com/zenithporto; Praça de Carlos Alberto 86; brunch from €6; ⊙10am-8pm Wed-Mon; 🛜) Funky brick-walled space for a blowout brunch and barista-made coffee. Nice people-watching terrace. Tuck into eggs Benedict, smashed avocado and crumbed poached eggs and the like. Cool can also mean crowded, so expect a wait to get in.

Traveller Caffé (Map p58, G4; Rua Passos Manuel 165; breakfast €5-9, snacks €5-7; ⊙8.15am-7pm Mon-Thu, to 9pm Fri & Sat, to 8pm Sun) Chilled traveller hang-out. Breakfasts are bang on the money, and range from Greek- and French-style options to açaí bowls with granola.

go thirsty at this boutique watering hole. Better still, it's located directly across the road from the jaw-droppingly beautiful Igreja do Carmo (decked head-to-toe in blue and white *azulejo* tiles). Choose from eight tap beers or let the staff suggest a bottle from the fridge. (www.facebook.com/cervejariadocarmo; Praça de Carlos Alberto 124; ⊙2pm-midnight Mon-Thu, to 1am Fri, to 2am Sat; 🛜)

Café Majestic
CAFE

33 🍽 MAP P58, G4

Yes, we know, it's pricey and rammed with tourists brandishing selfie sticks, but you should at least have a drink at Café Majestic just so you can gawp at its beaux arts interior, awash with prancing cherubs, opulently gilded woodwork

and gold-braided waiters. Skip the so-so food and just go for coffee. There's a pavement terrace for sunny-day people-watching. (www.cafemajestic.com; Rua de Santa Catarina 112; ⊙9.30am-11.30pm Mon-Sat)

Base
BAR

34 🍽 MAP P58, B5

On sunny days and warm nights, beeline to Base – one of Porto's coolest open-air bars, perched amid the olive trees of the Passeio dos Clérigos urban park. A mix of wooden benches, deckchairs and picnic rugs provide plenty of seating options on the manicured lawn and offer excellent views of Porto's iconic Clérigos Tower. (☎910 076 920; www.baseporto.com; Passeio dos Clérigos, Rua das Carmelitas; ⊙noon-9pm)

The Wall

BAR

35 MAP P58, C4

With backlit walls featuring a 3D cubist artwork of spirit bottles, high ceilings and a funky world map of names, the Wall has a dash of the urban sophisticate about it. Mingle with an effortlessly cool crowd enjoying the chilled DJ beats and expertly mixed cocktails (it boasts a mean mojito). (www.facebook.com/thewall bar.baixa; Rua de Cândido dos Reis 90; ⏱5pm-4am Mon-Sat, 9pm-4am Sun)

Duas de Letra

CAFE

36 MAP P58, H4

Artsy cafe overlooking a leafy square, with a low-key vibe, wooden ceilings, an exhibition space upstairs with rotating exhibits, and two patios. The snacks are delicious, and there's a great tea selection. The day special, including soup and a drink, goes for just €7. (www.duasdeletra.pt; Passeio de São Lázaro 48; ⏱10am-10pm Mon-Thu, to midnight Fri & Sat, 2-8pm Sun; 🛜)

Café Candelabro

CAFE

37 MAP P58, C2

Cool cafe-bar in a former bookstore, with a boho crowd and a retro vibe featuring black-and-white mosaic tile floors, bookcases with old books and magazines, and big windows opening out to the street. It gets busy with upbeat tunes and occasional gigs at weekends. (Rua da Conceição 3; ⏱10.30am-2am Mon-Fri, 4pm-2am Sat, 4pm-midnight Sun)

Aliados & Bolhão Drinking

Café Majestic (p68)

AGNIESZKA SKALSKA / SHUTTERSTOCK ©

The Potter in Porto

If you feel as though you've apparated to Diagon Alley as you duck through the lanes of old Porto at twilight, perhaps glimpsing the theatrical swish of a student's black cloak on the cobbles, you are not alone. There is, in fact, more than a pinch of Porto in Potter.

From 1991 to 1993, JK Rowling lived in Porto, busy scribbling the first draft of *Harry Potter and the Philosopher's Stone* in longhand by day, and working as an English teacher in a language institute in the evening. The city soon cast its spell on her, with its moodily lit alleyways, hidden corners and grand cafes – including one of her old haunts, Café Majestic (p68) – which look freshly minted for a Potter film set.

Step into the exuberant Livraria Lello (p60) and you can't help but think that its twisting staircase might open the door to some passageway or chamber. The neo-Gothic bookshop is pure fantasy stuff. It's crowded with tourists by day, so it's better to come in the early evening to really unlock its magic.

Casa do Livro   LOUNGE

38   MAP P58, B4

Vintage wallpaper, gilded mirrors and walls of books give a discreet charm to this nicely lit beer and wine bar. On weekends, DJs spin funk, soul, jazz and retro sounds in the back room. (www.facebook.com/casadolivroporto; Rua Galeria de Paris 85; 9.30pm-3am Sun-Thu, to 4am Fri & Sat)

Galeria de Paris   BAR

The original on the strip that's now synonymous with the Porto party scene (see 39 Map p58, B4), this whimsically decorated spot has toys, thermos flasks, old phones and other assorted memorabilia lining the walls. In addition to cocktails and draught beer, you'll find tapas at night. (www.facebook.com/restaurante galeriadeparis; Rua Galeria de Paris 56; 8.30am-3am Sun-Thu, to 4am Fri & Sat)

Café au Lait   BAR

39   MAP P58, B4

Housed in a former textile warehouse, this narrow, intimate bar now stitches together a lively and unpretentious artistic crowd. Besides cocktails, there are snacks and salads, including vegetarian grub. DJs and occasional gigs amp up the vibe and add to the good cheer. (www.facebook.com/aulait.cafe; Rua Galeria de Paris 46; 10pm-4am Tue-Sat)

Plano B   BAR

40   MAP P58, C4

Something of a Porto stalwart on the Rua Cândido dos Reis, Plano B is where DJs and live bands hold court. Much like the crowd, the line-up is truly eclectic, with performance art, theatre and art openings held regularly. (www.facebook.com/pg/planobclub; Rua Cândido dos Reis 30; ⏰10pm-6am Wed-Sat; 📶)

Livraria da Baixa CAFE

41 ⭐ MAP P58, C5

Part 1920s bookshop, part cafe-bar, this old-school charmer spills out onto the cobbled pavement – a terrific spot for people-watching and eavesdropping over tea or a glass of wine. (www.facebook.com/livrariadabaixa; Rua das Carmelitas 15; ⏰10am-2am; 📶)

Entertainment

Teatro Municipal Rivoli THEATRE

42 ⭐ MAP P58, E4

This art deco theatre is one of the linchpins of Porto's evolving cultural scene. It traverses the whole spectrum from theatre to music, contemporary circus, cinema, dance and marionette productions. (📞223 392 200; www.teatromunicipal-doporto.pt; Praça Dom João I; ♿)

Maus Hábitos PERFORMING ARTS

43 ⭐ MAP P58, G4

Maus Hábitos or 'Bad Habits' is an arty, nicely chilled haunt hosting a culturally ambitious agenda. Changing exhibitions and imaginative installations adorn the walls, while live bands and DJs work the small stage. (www.maushabitos.com; 4th fl, Rua Passos Manuel 178; ⏰noon-

midnight Tue, to 2am Wed & Thu, to 4am Fri & Sat, noon-5pm Sun)

Teatro Nacional São João THEATRE

44 ⭐ MAP P58, F6

The lavish, romantic Teatro Nacional São João was built in the style of Paris' Palais Garnier. One of Porto's premier performing-arts organisations, it hosts international dance, theatre and music groups. (📞223 401 900; www.tnsj.pt; Praça da Batalha)

Coliseu do Porto CONCERT VENUE

45 ⭐ MAP P58, G4

This frayed, yet still stylish, art deco theatre hosts major gigs as well as grand theatre and dance productions. If something big is going on down here, you'll see posters all over town. (📞223 394 940; www.coliseudoporto.pt; Rua Passos Manuel 137)

Shopping

Workshops Pop Up ARTS & CRAFTS

Bringing a new lease of life to a restored smithy (see 8 🔘 Map p58, C3), this store is the brainchild of Nuno and Rita. It harbours an eclectic mix of pop-ups selling everything from original ceramics to vintage fashion, accessories and prettily wrapped Bonjardim soaps. It also runs three-hour cookery workshops (p61), some of which are in English. (📞966 974 119; www.workshops-popup.com; Rua do Almada 275; ⏰1-7.30pm Sun-Fri, 10am-7.30pm Sat)

Craft Beer Cool

Riding the craft beer wave that is currently so big in Porto, **Armazém da Cerveja** (Map p58, H4; www.armazem.beer; Rua Formosa 130; ⏱4pm-midnight Tue-Thu & Sun, to 1am Fri & Sat) has 70 brews on offer (tripping the globe from Belgium to the States). A house lager will set you back just €1.50. There's a beer garden and, should you so wish, you can even bring along your own picnic.

A Pérola do Bolhão   FOOD & DRINKS

46 🅖 MAP P58, F3

Founded in 1917, this delightfully old-school deli sports Porto's most striking art nouveau facade and is stacked to the rafters with smoked sausages and pungent mountain cheeses, olives, dried fruits and nuts, wine and port. The beautiful *azulejos* (decorative tiles) depict flowers and two goddess-like women bearing *café* (coffee) and *chá* (tea) plants. (Rua Formosa 279; ⏱9.30am-7.30pm Mon-Fri, 9am-1pm Sat)

Coração Alecrim   ARTS & CRAFTS

47 🅖 MAP P58, B2

'Green, indie, vintage' is the strapline of this enticing store, accessed through a striking doorway painted with woodland animals (crickets chirrup a welcome as you enter). It stocks high-quality handmade Portuguese products, from purewool blankets and beanies to one-off *azulejos*, shell coasters and beautiful ceramics. (www.coracao alecrim.com; Travessa de Cedofeita 28; ⏱11am-7pm Mon-Sat)

Azulima   ARTS & CRAFTS

48 🅖 MAP P58, F1

Heaven for the *azulejo* obsessed, this shop does a fine line in tiles of every shape, size and colour – from geometric to naturalistic, from slick and modern to classic blue-and-white numbers. (www.azulima.pt; Rua do Bolhão 124; ⏱9.30am-12.30pm & 2.30-7pm Mon-Fri, 10am-12.30pm Sat)

águas furtadas   ARTS, FASHION

49 🅖 MAP P58, C4

This boutique is a treasure trove of funky Portuguese fashion, design, crafts and accessories, including born-again Barcelos cockerels in candy-bright colours and exquisitely illustrated pieces by influential Porto-based graphic designer Benedita Feijó. (www.facebook.com/aguasfurtadas; Rua do Almada 13; ⏱10am-7.30pm Mon-Sat, 1-7pm Sun)

Livraria Latina   BOOKS

50 🅖 MAP P58, F5

This beautiful old bookstore first opened its doors in 1942, making it one of Porto's oldest. Pop in for a great collection of Portuguese literature, as well as a solid selection of foreign-language titles. (Rua de Santa Catarina 2; ⏱9am-7.30pm Mon-Fri, to 7pm Sat)

Touriga
WINE

51 MAP P58, C4

Run with passion and precision by David Ferreira, this fabulous wine shop is a trove of well- and lesser-known ports and wines – many from small producers. Stop by for a wine or port-wine tasting (€5 to €20). Shipping can be arranged. (📞 225 108 435; Rua da Fábrica 32; 🕙10am-8pm Mon-Sat)

Vista Alegre
CERAMICS

52 MAP P58, C5

Vista Alegre has been doing the finest line in Portuguese porcelain since 1824, with pieces ranging from minimalist to those emblazoned with naturalistic motifs. (Rua das Carmelitas 40; 🕙10am-8pm Mon-Sat)

Casa Ramos
FOOD

53 MAP P58, F3

Old-world grocery stores like this one are a dying breed. Besides beans, *bacalhau* and *alheira* sausages by the kilo, you'll find everything from traditional sweets to teas and charcuterie here. (Rua Sá da Bandeira 347; 🕙9am-7pm Mon-Fri, to 1pm Sat)

Louie Louie
MUSIC

54 MAP P58, D1

Click into the groove of retro Porto at Louie Louie, well stocked with vinyl and secondhand CDs to whisk you through the entire musical spectrum – from reggae and rock to hip hop, soul, funk, disco, jazz, punk and Portuguese fado. It's cheap and cheerful. (www.louielouie.biz; Rua do Almada 536; 🕙10.30am-7pm Mon-Sat)

Aliados & Bolhão Shopping

A Pérola do Bolhão (p72)

MEHUL PATEL / AGE FOTOSTOCK ©

Porto's Street Art Scene

If only walls could speak... Well, in Porto they do – volumes. The narrative is of Porto's growing tribe of street artists, whose bold, eye-catching works emblazon facades. Hurled across crumbling ancient walls, empty storefront glass and neglected stucco, they lend artistic edge, urban grit and an element of the unexpected to the everyday. A far cry from graffiti scrawls, the spray-paint wonders reveal artistic flair and creative expression that transcend the conventional and stop you dead in your tracks.

Porto-born or -based artists include the startlingly prolific Hazul Luzah (a pseudonym), who works incognito under the cloak of darkness. His naturalistic, geometric-patterned, curlicue-embellished works dance across dilapidated city walls in the shape of flowers, exotic birds or religious motifs. Other home-grown talent includes Costah, known for his playful, brightly coloured murals; Frederico Draw, master of striking black-and-white graffiti portraits; and the ever-inventive Mr Dheo. Some of the artists are self-taught, others have backgrounds in architecture, digital art, illustration and design.

To plug into the scene today, arrange your own self-guided tour of Porto's must-see street art. High on any list should be the Travessa de Cedofeita and Escadas do Codeçal, as well as the car park at Trindade, with its large-scale, in-your-face murals. Lapa, just one metro stop north, is another hotspot, as is the gallery-dotted Rua Miguel Bombarda. On Rua das Flores, clever graffiti sits side by side with beautifully restored historic buildings – look out for vibrantly patterned works by Hazul, glowing neon portraits by Costah and 15 electric boxes – each with its own burst of street-art colour. In Miragaia, check out the facade of Look at Porto (p117), where urban artist Alexandre Farto (or Vhils) has scratched the surface to create a one-of-a-kind portrait that gazes out towards the river.

For anyone serious about street art, it's also worth seeing Rua Lionesa, north of the centre in Leça do Balio. It's a giant canvas for the murals of 10 well-known street artists – Frederico Draw and Mr Dheo included – and proof that the passion for this urban art form knows no bounds.

Casa Chinesa

55 🔒 MAP P58, F3   FOOD

This delightfully old-fashioned emporium is crammed with traditional Portuguese products – sardines, sausages, dried cod and octopus, *broa de Avintes* (dense corn and rye flatbread), piri-piri chilli peppers – you name it. It's also a good

ACMETRAVELLER PORTO / ALAMY STOCK PHOTO ©

Chocolates from Arcádia

spot to stock up on nuts, grains, gluten-free, vegetarian and Asian ingredients. (Rua Sá da Bandeira 343; ⊙9am-1pm & 3-7.30pm Mon-Fri, to 1pm Sat)

Arcádia
CHOCOLATE

56 🔒 MAP P58, C4

Purveyors of handcrafted chocolates, Arcádia has been reeling in the sweet-toothed locals since 1933. This gloriously old-fashioned shop rolls out gift-boxed pralines and flavoured bonbons, cocoa-rich bars, chocolates with Calém port or in the delicate form of hearts and flowers, and almond liqueur dragées – all made with care to

traditional recipes. (www.arcadia. pt; Rua do Almada 63; ⊙9.30am-7pm Mon-Fri, to 5.30pm Sat)

A Vida Portuguesa
GIFTS & SOUVENIRS

57 🔒 MAP P58, B4

This lovely store in an old fabric shop showcases a medley of stylishly repackaged vintage Portuguese products – classic toys, old-fashioned soaps and retro journals, plus those emblematic ceramic Bordallo Pinheiro andorinhas (swallows). (www.avidaportuguesa. com; Rua Galeria de Paris 20; ⊙10am-8pm Mon-Sat, 11am-7pm Sun)

Walking Tour 🚶

Galerias Bar Crawl

Ask a tripeiro where the party is and chances are they'll direct you towards the Galerias, the nightlife hub around Rua Galeria de Paris and Rua Cândido dos Reis in the Aliados & Bolhão neighbourhood. Swinging from retro to boho, urban-cool to alternative, the bars are as busy as beehives at weekends, with the fun spilling out onto the streets. Bar-crawling is the way to go – simply follow your mood.

Walk Facts

Start The Wall

End Era uma Vez em Paris

Length 300m; as long as the night lasts

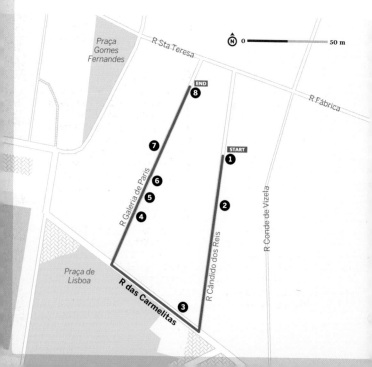

❶ Urban Cool

Bottles of spirits glow on the funkily backlit, 3D walls at **The Wall** (p69), which is bouncing on weekend nights. It's a cool and contemporary lounge bar in which to kick off a big evening. Go for an excellent cocktail (or two) and cool music.

❷ Party Plans

Mosey a little further along Rua Cândido dos Reis and you'll stumble across **Plano B** (p70), where the party spreads across two floors and DJs pump out everything from electro to house and RnB. Gigs and events from exhibition launches to performance art also feature.

❸ Retro Bookshop

If you're seeking a slightly more retro vibe, head across to nearby **Livraria da Baixa** (p71), an intimate, vintage-cool space in a former 1920s bookshop for drinks and conversing by candlelight. There's a street terrace for warm-weather imbibing.

❹ Boho Hang-Out

Turn the corner onto Rua Galeria de Paris and you hit the super-slick, Scandi-style **La Bohème** (p67), with its bare pine interior designed by AVA Architects. It's a nicely chilled spot to sample Portuguese wines and tapas.

❺ Warehouse Welcome

Both gay and straight, **Café au Lait** (p70) lodges in a former textile warehouse. It now draws a sociable, down-to-earth crowd with its upbeat jazz, blues and soul tunes, decent DJ line-up and reasonably priced drinks.

❻ Strip Original

Still rocking it many years on, **Galeria de Paris** (p70) is an old curiosity shop of a bar on the main party mile. Its wooden display cabinets are crammed with vintage knick-knacks raided from many attics. Go for the drinks and good vibes on weekends when it's in full swing.

❼ Highballs & DJs

Just a couple of steps away is hip 'n' happening **Casa do Livro** (p70), another classic on Porto's after-dark scene. Antique furniture, gilded mirrors, a pinstriped wall and book-lined shelves set the scene in the low-lit bookstore-turned-bar. Sip a highball as DJs spin house and soul.

❽ 1920s Paris

Parisian flair meets Porto at **Era uma Vez em Paris** (p66), a throwback to the more wildly glamorous 1920s, with its vintage furnishings, red walls and lamps casting flickering shadows. Gigs, DJs and the coolest of cocktails end your night on a boho-style high.

SALUTIS
ERICULIS

Explore ⊕

Miragaia

Sloping down to the riverside – its brightly painted, laundry-strung houses pasted picturesquely to the hillside – Miragaia is a delight for a serendipitous wander. Besides a handful of sights and an art-crammed gallery, the real appeal here is strolling labyrinthine lanes to sky-high viewpoints, time-warp bars and family-run tascas (taverns) in the old Jewish quarter, Vitória. Here history waits around every cobbled corner.

Make a beeline for Museu Nacional Soares dos Reis (p80) to take in its prized decorative and fine arts collection. Revive gallery-weary eyes over coffee or an organic, season-driven lunch at nearby Época (p89).

Now turn your focus to the free, jail-turned-photography museum Centro Português de Fotografia (p82). From here, slip into the former Jewish quarter. Following the highly atmospheric Rua de São Bento da Vitória (p85) brings you to the Igreja Nossa Senhora da Vitória (p88).

As evening draws in, see the city spread out before you at Miradouro da Vitória (p85), then join a cool crowd for wine and jazz at roof terrace Mirajazz (p93).

Getting There & Around

Ⓜ **Metro** Stops include Aliados and São Bento.

🚊 **Tram** Tram 1 (Infante–Passeio Alegre) trundles along the riverfront, connecting the city centre to Foz do Douro, stopping at Alfândega en route.

Miragaia Map on p86

Azulejos (hand-painted tiles), Igreja do Carmo (p88)
FOTOKON / GETTY IMAGES ©

Top Sight 📷
Museu Nacional Soares dos Reis

Museu Nacional Soares dos Reis' stellar collection swings from Neolithic carvings to Dutch master-pieces in the ornate Palácio das Carrancas. Requisitioned by Napoleonic invaders, the neo-classical palace was abandoned so rapidly that the future Duke of Wellington found an unfinished banquet in the dining hall. Most striking of all are 19th-century sculptures by namesake António Soares dos Reis and António Teixeira Lopes.

◉ MAP P86, B3

www.museusoares
dosreis.pt

Rua Dom Manuel II 44

adult/child €5/free

🕙10am-6pm Tue-Sun

António Soares dos Reis Gallery

The museum prides itself on its works by lauded 19th-century Portuguese sculptor António Soares dos Reis. Top billing goes to *O Desterrado* (The Exiled), which is considered the apogee of Portuguese sculpture. Sculpted in Carrara marble in Rome in 1872, this man with a wistful gaze was inspired by a poem of exile by Alexandre Herculano.

Sculpture Collection

Soares dos Reis' sculptures share the limelight with other notable works by 19th- and 20th-century Portuguese masters. Among them is the pensive *Childhood of Cain* (1890) by António Teixeira Lopes, Augusto Santo's *Ismael* (1889) and Diogo de Macedo's bronze *Boy's Head* (1927). Much older is the 3rd-century BC Roman sarcophagus, embellished with a frieze alluding to the four seasons.

Painting Collection

The painting collection takes a chronological romp through 2500 pieces from the 16th to the 20th centuries, homing in on Portuguese, Dutch and Flemish portraiture, landscapes and religious works. Romanticism and Naturalism predominate. Star works to look out for include Francisco Vieira's evocative *Flight of Margaret of Anjou*, Joaquim Vitorino Ribeiro's serene *Christian Martyr* and Henrique Pousão's chiaroscuro *Woman Dressed in Black*.

Decorative Arts

The 2nd floor showcases decorative arts. Besides fine examples of Portuguese 17th-century faience and 18th-century Chinese porcelain, you'll find intricate 19th-century glassware by Vista Alegre, jewellery (from Iron Age to delicate 18th-century Portuguese filigree creations) and 17th-century Namban screens, which vividly portray the arrival of Portuguese colonisers on Japanese shores.

★ Top Tips

o Stop by the shop for quality gifts and the library to buff up on your art history.

o Don't miss the António Soares dos Reis Gallery, paintings by Portuguese, Dutch and Flemish masters, and the sculpture by António Teixeira Lopes.

✕ Take a Break

The museum's tranquil cafe (p91) does decent and inexpensive lunch specials (there's always a vegetarian option).

Or nip around the corner to Scandicool Época (p89) for terrific coffee and a light bite to eat.

Top Sight

Centro Português de Fotografia

Standing sentinel on the edge of Porto's former Jewish quarter, this muscular edifice, built in 1767, was both a prison and a court of appeal in former lives. With the Carnation Revolution and the fall of dictatorship in 1974, it ceased to be a jail. Nowadays it is an eerie, highly atmospheric backdrop for rotating photography exhibitions – many with a thought-provoking slant.

⊙ MAP P86, E6

Portuguese Photography Centre

www.cpf.pt

Campo dos Mártires da Pátria

admission free

🕙 10am-6pm Tue-Fri, 3-7pm Sat & Sun

Architecture & History

You can sense the weight of history as you wander through the complex. The former cells, including one where prominent 19th-century Portuguese writer Camilo Castelo Branco was holed up from 1860 to 1861 (adultery was his crime, for the record), are now given over to exhibitions. But the sepia photos of one-time inmates are a nod to its grim past, as are the impenetrable walls and metal grilles.

Photography Exhibitions

The centre hosts a number of photography exhibitions each year – from portraiture to provocative themes, the abstract to the landscape. Exhibitions zooming in on subjects such as abandonment and ruined buildings, war-torn landscapes, and the unpublished photographs of Frida Kahlo have recently featured.

Camera Collection

A blast from a sepia-tinted past, the permanent collection of old cameras (pictured left) in the top-floor museum harks back to the early beginnings of photography. In an Instagram age, it's a reminder of how laborious photography once was. Photography fans are in their element taking in Kodak detective cameras, early-20th-century Brownies, Century, Varsity and Goldy wonders, early 1930s SLRs and more.

Photography Excursion

Inspired? Why not use your new-found inspiration to take some great photos of your own? Duck down the medieval lanes fanning out from Rua de São Bento da Vitória (p85) for street-life shots. Or capture the cityscape during the day and at dusk from the nearby Miradouro da Vitória (p85).

★ Top Tips

○ Entry is free, so come and go as you please.

○ Factor in time for a wander in the alley-woven old Jewish quarter nearby.

○ Look out for the far-from-compact 1900 Penrose Process Camera, one of the largest in the world.

○ Check out the selection of international books and magazines in the library.

✕ Take a Break

A pleasant five-minute walk through Jardim da Cordoaria brings you to Noshi Coffee (p90) for great coffee and healthy snacks from toasties to salads.

Fill up on good, honest Portuguese home cooking at family-run O Caraças (p91) on nearby Rua das Taipas.

Miragaia Centro Português de Fotografia

Walking Tour 🥾

Jewish Porto

The tight skein of medieval alleyways around Rua de São Bento da Vitória was once the beating heart of the Jewish quarter of Olival, which grew up in the 14th century. Jews made up a third of Porto's population back then, but their numbers dwindled dramatically after the Inquisition. Dip into the neighbourhood's backstreets to find out more about this remarkable chapter in Porto's history.

Walk Facts

Start Rua de São Bento da Vitória

End Mirajazz

Length 650m; one hour

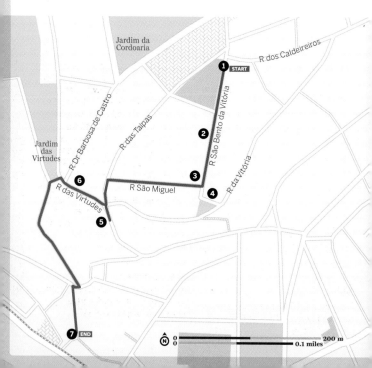

❶ Medieval Charm

With its pretty tiled houses with wrought-iron balconies and cobbles polished smooth by centuries of shoe leather, the narrow, gently curving **Rua de São Bento da Vitória** was the beating heart of Jewish Porto in late medieval times. Keep your eyes peeled for telltale sights of Jewish heritage, such as bronze Hamsa (protective hand) door knockers.

❷ Monastic Life

Note the sign in front of former monastery **Mosteiro de São Bento da Vitória** (Rua de São Bento da Vitória) apologising for the expulsion of the Jews in 1496 under the Portuguese Inquisition and the iron fist of King Manuel I. Classified a National Monument, it harbours a beautiful granite cloister and stages performances by the Teatro Nacional de São João (p94).

❸ Azulejo Panel

As you amble down the hill, keep a lookout on the right-hand side for the **Casa da Rua São Miguel** (Rua São Miguel 4). On the corner, at No. 4, you'll see a panel of 19th-century blue, white and yellow-trim *azulejos* (hand-painted tiles) showing scenes from the life of the Virgin and of everyday life in Porto.

❹ Heavenly Views

For knockout views over Porto's tumbledown rooftops to the graceful arc of the bridge over the river, stop by hilltop **Miradouro da Vitória** (Rua São Bento da Vitória). It's a highly atmospheric spot at dusk when the landmarks are illuminated and the lights on Vila Nova de Gaia's wine lodges flick on one by one.

❺ Communal Fountain

One of Porto's handful of remaining public fountains, which were once a place to tap into fresh spring water and local gossip, the stone-carved, neoclassical-style **Chafariz da Rua das Taipas** (Rua das Taipas) dates to the late 18th century.

❻ Local Lunch

Swing around the corner and more marvellous views of the city unfold as your path dips down to Miragaia from the Jardim das Virtudes. On the corner is family-run tavern **Taberna de Santo António** (🖉 222 055 306; Rua das Virtudes 32; mains €8.50-12; ⏰noon-3pm & 7-10pm Tue-Sun), which prides itself on serving up honest Portuguese grub with a smile. It dishes up generous helpings of codfish, grilled sardines and *cozido* (meat and vegetable stew) to the lunchtime crowds.

❼ Roof Terrace

After a satisfying lunch, where better to slip into a relaxed evening than over cool drinks and jazzy beats at **Mirajazz** (p93)?

Miragaia

N

0 200 m
0 0.1 miles

CEDOFEITA

R da Boa Nova
R do Breiner
R do Breiner
R de Adolfo Casais Monteiro
R do Rosário
R Miguel Bombarda
R de Cedofeita
Tv de Cedofeita
Tv do Carregal
Tv do Carregal
R Prof. Jaime Rios de Sousa

Capela
Incomum

Jardim do
Carregal

R Prof Vicente J Carvalho

R Dr T Almeida

R Alberto
A Gouveia

R Dom Manuel II

Museu Nacional
Soares dos Reis

R José Falcão

R S.ta Teresa

R Ceuta

R S.ta Noronha

Praça
Gomes
Fernandes

Praça
Carlos
Alberto

Igreja do
Carmo

Igreja das
Carmelitas

Praça Gomes
Teixeira

R Galeria de Paris

R das Carmelitas

R Cândido dos Reis

Praça de
Lisboa

Praça
Parada
Leitão

R do Carmo

Tv do Carmo

R da Restauração

27
32
21
16
17
10
25
33
13
2
1
26
29

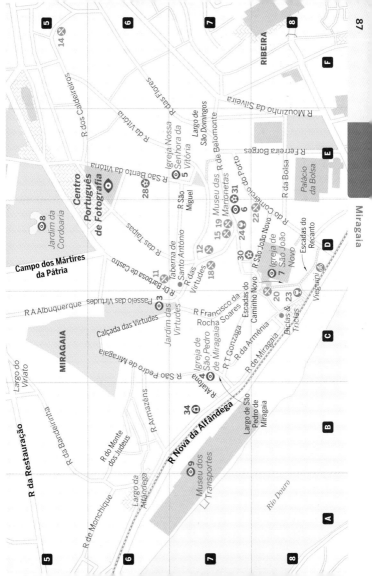

Sights

Igreja das Carmelitas CHURCH

1 ⊙ MAP P86, D4

Blink and you might miss that this is a church in its own right, snuggled as close as it is to the Igreja do Carmo. The twin churches are separated only by a 1m-wide house, once the dividing line between the monks of Carmo and the Carmelite nuns. Dating to the 17th century, its modest classical facade belies its lavishly gilded nave. (Rua do Carmo; ⊙7.30am-7pm Mon-Fri, 9am-6.45pm Sat & Sun)

Igreja do Carmo CHURCH

2 ⊙ MAP P86, D4

Dating to the late 18th century, this captivating *azulejo*-covered church is one of Porto's best examples of rococo architecture. The tiled panel on the facade pays tribute to Nossa Senhora (Our Lady). (Rua do Carmo; ⊙8am-noon & 1-6pm Mon & Wed, 9am-6pm Tue & Thu, to 5.30pm Fri, to 4pm Sat, to 1.30pm Sun)

Jardim das Virtudes GARDENS

3 ⊙ MAP P86, C6

A much-loved picnic spot of *trip-eiros*, these tucked-away gardens stagger down the hillside in a series of lawn terraces. Find a shady spot under the trees to drink in the far-reaching views across the city, which stretch over the rooftops, down to the river and up to the port lodges in Vila Nova de Gaia. (Passeio das Virtudes; ⊙9am-7pm)

Igreja de São Pedro de Miragaia CHURCH

4 ⊙ MAP P86, B7

One of Porto's oldest churches, the medieval Igreja de São Pedro de Miragaia was completely rebuilt in the 17th and 18th centuries, and pays homage to St Peter, patron saint of fishermen. Its exterior is beautifully tiled with blue and white *azulejos*, which segue into its light interior. The altar is a profusion of intricate gilded woodcarvings. (Largo de São Pedro de Miragaia; ⊙3.30-7pm Tue-Sat, 10-11.30am Sun)

Igreja Nossa Senhora da Vitória CHURCH

5 ⊙ MAP P86, E7

In Porto's medieval Vitória quarter, this church stands on land that once belonged to the Jewish community. Completed in 1539, it was given a baroque makeover in the 18th century following a devastating fire, and features impressive woodcarvings from this period. The Nossa Senhora da Vitória (Blessed Virgin Mary) sculpture in the altar is the handiwork of feted sculptor Soares dos Reis. (Rua São Bento da Vitória 1; ⊙9am-noon & 4-7.30pm Tue-Fri, 9am-noon & 2.30-5pm Sat, 9am-11.30pm Sun)

Museu das Marionetas MUSEUM

6 ⊙ MAP P86, D7

Porto's marionette museum turns the spotlight on the remarkable puppet creations that have taken to the stage at the Teatro Marionetas do Porto (p95) over the past 25 years. Rotating exhibitions present marionettes from productions such as *Macbeth*, *Faust* and *Cinderella*. (www.marionetasdoporto.pt; Rua de Belomonte 61; admission €2; ⏲11am-1pm & 2-6pm; 🚹)

Igreja de São João Novo   CHURCH

7 ◎ MAP P86, D8

Set up above a narrow maze of stone stairs, this medieval church with magnificent views was built in 1539 on land that was originally part of Porto's old Jewish quarter. It's a nice place to stop, take a breath and listen to sad fado tunes riding the wind. (Largo de São João Novo; ⏲8-11am & 3-5pm Mon-Fri, 4.30-6.30pm Sat, 8-10am Sun)

Jardim da Cordoaria   PARK

8 ◎ MAP P86, D5

This pleasantly leafy park is known simply as 'Cordoaria'. Check out the four haunting sculptures by Spanish sculptor Juan Muñoz. The romantic, narrow lanes that run north from the Cordoaria are the domain of Porto's hippest bars. (Rua Campo dos Mártires da Pátria)

Museu dos Transportes   MUSEUM

9 ◎ MAP P86, B7

Set in the 19th-century riverside customs house, this museum traces the motorcar from its inception to the future. It does the same for radio and telecommunications. (www.amtc.pt; Rua Nova da Alfândega;

Get on Your Bike

Biclas & Triclas (Map p86, C8; ☎220 996 130; www.tricla.pt; Rua da Arménia 30; full-day rentals €10; ⏲9.30am-8pm) is conveniently located on the banks of the Douro, meaning you don't have to tackle any hills to reach the riverside cycle paths (although electric bikes to help conquer said hills are available). A number of tours are also offered that combine cycling with surfing, eating and drinking (not at the same time).

automobile exhibition adult/child €3/1.50, communications exhibition €5/2.50; ⏲10am-1pm & 2-6pm Tue-Fri, 3-7pm Sat & Sun)

Eating

Época   CAFE €

10 🍴 MAP P86, B3

This sunlit cafe rocks the Scandinavian look with light timber furniture and fresh white walls. As well as doling out the rich juices of coffee beans, Época also caters to the vegan and vegetarian market with its rotating menu of veggie-friendly dishes. Check the blackboard behind the counter for specials, and know the couple in charge make everything with love. (☎913 732 038; www.epocaporto.com; Rua do Rosário 22; breakfasts from €3.50; ⏲9am-5pm Tue-Fri, 10am-4pm Sat; 🌱)

Miragaia Eating

Porto's Tripeiros

Spend any length of time in Porto and you'll notice that even locals affectionately refer to each other as *tripeiros*, which literally translates as a seller or eater of tripe. But why?

One theory refers to the Age of Discovery in the 14th and 15th centuries when Porto, like much of Portugal, ruled the colonial waves of exploration. Lore has it that the navigators took the best cuts of meat for their lengthy voyages and left behind nothing but offal for the locals. Others swear that the name has its roots from the Portuguese Civil War (1828–34) and the Siege of Porto in 1832, when all the good meat went to the soldiers and nothing but tripe was left for the residents.

One thing is certain, tripe still stars on many a restaurant menu in the form of *tripas à moda do Porto*, a hearty tripe, vegetable and white bean stew, seasoned with bay leaves, lemon, garlic and coriander, and mopped up with crusty bread – it's Porto comfort food par excellence.

Porta 4   TAPAS €

11 ⓧ MAP P86, D6

The clue's in the name: Porta 4 has just four tables for a lucky handful of diners, so book ahead. If you can snag one of them, you're in for a treat: this enticingly cosy cubbyhole turns out bang-on-the-money *petiscos* (tapas), from squid with green apple and basil to pork loin with beetroot polenta – all at €5 a pop. (📞913 203 489; Rua do Dr Barbosa de Castro 4; petiscos €5, chef's menu for 2 people €30; ⏱7.30-11.30pm Mon-Sat)

Hungry Biker   CAFE €

12 ⓧ MAP P86, D7

If you – like the husband and wife owners – love to ride your bicycle, this place is a winner. The artsy cafe has an environmentally friendly ethos, decked out with furniture

fashioned from reclaimed wooden pallets and old doors. Go for luxe breakfasts, brunches (superfood toasts, homemade waffles...) or a vitamin-packed smoothie. Bike rental costs €4/11 per half-/full day. (Rua das Taipas 68-72; breakfast & light bites €2.50-7; ⏱9am-4pm)

Noshi Coffee   CAFE €

13 ⓧ MAP P86, D4

Noshi is a hip and healthy cafe with a welcoming atmosphere. You'll find a good coffee selection, including cappuccinos, soy lattes, 100% Arábica espressos and filter coffees. The food menu includes open toasties topped with combos like pear, chèvre cheese, honey and nuts, or avocado, mozzarella and dried chilli. There are also salads and pasta, plus gluten-free options. (📞222 053 034; www.facebook.com/noshicoffee;

Rua do Carmo 11; mains €7-11, lunch menu €8.90; 8.30am-7.30pm Tue-Fri, 9am-8pm Sat, 10am-6pm Sun; 📶)

A Sandeira

SANDWICHES €

14 🗺 MAP P86, F5

Charming, boho-flavoured and lit by fairy lights, A Sandeira is a great bolthole for an inexpensive lunch. Chipper staff bring to the table creative salads such as smoked ham, rocket, avocado and walnuts, and Porto's best sandwiches (olive, feta, tomato and basil, for instance). The lunch menu including soup, a salad or sandwich and a drink is a steal. (📞223 216 471; www.asandeira. pt; Rua dos Caldeireiros 85; sandwiches €4.90, lunch menu €5; 9am-midnight Mon-Sat; 📶)

El Argento

CAFE €

15 🗺 MAP P86, D7

At this dedicated *empanada* bar you can choose from a range of homemade pastry pockets packed with fillings like spicy chicken and provolone cheese, then side them with chunky *chimichurri* sauce. There are also sweet snacks like cakes and tarts, plus Argentinian wine and fresh-squeezed juices. (📞222 058 036; www.facebook.com/elargentoporto; Rua das Taipas 4; empanadas €2; noon-9.30pm Mon-Thu, to 10.30pm Fri & Sat)

Casa Diogo

CAFE €

16 🗺 MAP P86, A2

The Diogo family welcomes guests into this cafe like it's their home,

and the fact that the space is a renovated house with tables split across three rooms adds to the homeliness. A daily lunch menu includes traditional home-cooked food, and all bread, biscuits and cakes are made at the family's sixth-generation bakery outside Porto. (📞220 167 295; www.facebook.com/casadiogobiscoitariaemercearia fina; Rua de Miguel Bombarda 416; set lunch menu €6.50; 11am-7.30pm Mon-Thu, to 10pm Fri & Sat)

Museu Nacional Soares dos Reis Cafe

CAFE €

17 🗺 MAP P86, B3

The museum's tranquil cafe is a fine spot for a lunch special (there's always a vegetarian option) or come to linger over a coffee and slice of homemade tart. It opens onto a patio in summer. (www.museusoaresdosreis.pt; Rua Dom Manuel II; lunch specials €5.50-7.50; noon-6pm Tue, 10am-6pm Wed-Sun)

O Caraças

PORTUGUESE €

18 🗺 MAP P86, D7

Run with heart and soul by a mother and her two daughters, this quaint stone-walled tavern is a homely gem. There's no menu per se, but generous helpings of market-fresh Portuguese soul food – from salt cod to perfectly cooked pork – often feature. (📞222 017 179, 220 174 505; Rua das Taipas 27; mains €7-10; 11.30am-2.30pm & 7.30-11pm Mon-Sat)

Holy Spirits

Tucked down a backstreet off the shopping street Rua de Cedofeita, **Capela Incomum** (Map p86, D2; 936 129 050; www.facebook.com/capelaincomum; Travessa do Carregal 77; glass of wine from €3; 4pm-midnight Mon-Wed, to 2am Thu-Sat) is a 19th-century chapel that was reborn as a classy two-storey wine bar when owner Francisa Lobão decided to put a shining light on Portugal's impressive selection of wines. Take note of the gorgeous wooden altar before heading upstairs to the quaint dining room for a platter of local meats and cheeses.

Belos Aires
ARGENTINE €€

19 MAP P86, D7

At the heart of this intimate part-Argentine, part-Portuguese restaurant is Mauricio, a chef with a big personality and an insatiable passion for his homeland, revealed as you watch him dashing around in the open kitchen. The market-fresh menu changes frequently, but you'll always find superb steaks and to-die-for *empanadas* (savoury turnovers). Save an inch for the chocolate brownie with *dulce de leche*. (223 195 661; www.facebook.com/belosairesrestaurante; Rua de Belomonte 104; mains €17-25; 8-11.30am & 7pm-midnight Mon-Sat;)

Intrigo
PORTUGUESE €€

20 MAP P86, C8

What's not to love about the sensational views over the rooftops and down to the river from the terrace of this tucked-away cafe, fitted out with a mishmash of vintage furnishings? Reached via a flight of steps, it puts its own riff on Portuguese flavours: from salt-cod fritters with grape jam to slow-cooked black pork cheek with sheep's cheese. (969 290 539; www.facebook.com/intrigobreadandsoul; Rua Tomás Gonzaga 90; mains €10-18; noon-10pm Sun-Thu, to 11pm Fri & Sat)

Frida
MEXICAN €€

21 MAP P86, A2

Named after the most flamboyant of Mexican painters, this restaurant spices up Porto's epicurean scene. Soft lamplight and walls plastered with Mexican newspaper cuttings and bold Frida Kahlo artworks create an intimate backdrop for punchy flavours ranging from beef tacos to *chile en nogada* (stuffed poblano chillies with walnut sauce) and zingy tequila-based cocktails. (226 062 286; www.cocinamestiza.pt; Rua Adolfo Casais Monteiro 135; mains €12-20; 8pm-midnight;)

Mistu
INTERNATIONAL €€€

22 MAP P86, D8

The marble bistro tables, Thonet chairs, soft lighting, arched windows and creeping foliage at cool Mistu are redolent of a more graceful age. Two friends transformed a neo-Moorish building into this intimate space, where the delicious food has Asian and South American overtones. Choose from dishes such as ceviche of tuna, ginger and avocado, or Thai-style prawns and *dulce de leche* fondant. (☎926 682 620; http://mistu.pt; Rua do Comércio do Porto 161; mains €19-28; ⊙8-11.30pm Mon, 12.30-3pm & 8-11.30pm Tue-Sat)

Drinking

Mirajazz WINE BAR

23 🚇 MAP P86, C8

Up the steep flight of steps from the river is one of the finest roof terraces in Porto: Mirajazz. Sunset is prime time for sipping a *porto*

tónico or a glass of well-chosen Portuguese wine and nibbling on predinner *petiscos* (tapas). The vibe is chilled, the music jazzy. (www.facebook.com/mirajazz; Escadas do Caminho Novo 11; ⊙3-8pm)

Pinguim Café BAR

24 🚇 MAP P86, D7

A little bubble of bohemian warmth in the heart of Porto, Pinguim attracts an alternative crowd. Stone walls and dim lighting create a cosy, intimate backdrop for plays, film screenings, poetry readings, rotating exhibitions of local art and G&T sipping. It's full to the rafters at weekends. (www.facebook.com/PinguimCafe; Rua de Belomonte 65; ⊙9pm-4am Mon-Fri, 10pm-4am Sat & Sun)

Catraio (p94)

EMILY MCAULIFFE / LONELY PLANET ©

Espiga   BAR

25 🅟 MAP P86, C3

Espiga is a cultural hub in Porto that blends food and drink with art and education. As a space to fuel the imagination, the cafe/bar/gallery hosts rotating exhibitions, workshops and other events (check Facebook for announcements). Brushed-concrete walls and pillars give a cool industrial feel, and the sunny terrace provides a top spot for chilling on a summer's afternoon. (📞 934 214 308; www.facebook.com/espigagaleriabar; Rua Clemente Menéres 65A; spirits & cocktails from €4; ⏱ 4pm-1am Wed-Sun)

Catraio   BAR

26 🅟 MAP P86, D1

Bottle lights illuminate this sleek bar and shop combo.The emphasis is on Portuguese craft beers, but there's also a solid global selection – with brews from everywhere from the Czech Republic to the US. (https://catraio.pt; Rua de Cedofeita 256; ⏱ 4pm-midnight Tue-Thu, to 2am Fri & Sat; 📶)

Gato Vadio   BAR

27 🅟 MAP P86, B1

Tucked behind a bookshop, this artistic cafe-bar run by a cultural association hosts film screenings, readings and occasional dinner parties. There's a nice little patio out the back, and it serves cakes, cookies and teas, and has a full bar. (www.gatovadiolivraria.blogspot.

com.au; Rua do Rosário 281; ⏱ 5pm-midnight Thu-Sun)

Entertainment

Teatro Nacional
São João   THEATRE

28 ⭐ MAP P86, E6

Few theatre backdrops are more atmospheric than the Mosteiro de São Bento da Vitória, which harbours an offshoot of the Teatro Nacional São João. See the website for the full line-up, which traverses the cultural spectrum from plays to ballet and readings. Tickets generally cost between €7.50 and €15. (📞 223 401 900; www.tnsj.pt; Rua de São Bento da Vitória)

Breyner 85   LIVE MUSIC

29 ⭐ MAP P86, C1

This creative space in a two-floor town house features an eclectic line-up of bands covering rock, jazz and blues, as well as DJ nights, karaoke and pub quizzes. The large grassy terrace is a treat. Popular Sunday jam sessions start at 11pm and entry is free, apart from a €3 minimum spend. (📞 936 440 865; www.breyner85.com; Rua do Breiner 85; ⏱ 7pm-2am Wed-Sun)

O Fado   FADO

30 ⭐ MAP P86, D7

Porto has no fado tradition of its own, but you can enjoy the Lisbon or Coimbra version of 'Portugal blues' into the wee hours at Restaurante O Fado. It's a tad touristy, but the fado is good. Mains will set you back between €23.50 and €45. (☎222 026 937; www.ofado.com; Largo de São João Novo 16; ⏰8.30pm-1am Mon-Sat)

Teatro Marionetas do Porto
THEATRE

31 ⭐ MAP P86, E7

A sure-fire hit with the kids (but not only aimed at children), this puppet theatre specialises in shows that range from fairy tales, such as Cinderella, to nonviolent political theatre. (☎222 089 175; www.marionetasdoporto.pt; Rua de Belmonte 57)

Shopping

Scar-id Store
CLOTHING

32 🔒 MAP P86, B1

This modern concept store is rightfully positioned in the midst of Porto's art district, where it showcases the wares of Portuguese designers. Owners André Ramos and Silvia Costa wanted to create a public outlet for the work of Porto's fashion talent, so began curating a unique range of clothing, jewellery, shoes and skincare that now includes products from around 40 designers. (www.scar-id.com; Rua do Rosário 253; ⏰3-8pm Mon, 10am-8pm Tue-Sat)

Garrafeira do Carmo
WINE

33 🔒 MAP P86, D4

Friendly, highly knowledgeable and attentive staff guide you through a

Hazul Street Art

Plug into Porto's street-art scene by taking a wander along Rua São Pedro de Miragaia. Here Hazul Luzah, one of Porto's most prolific street artists, who always works incognito, has jazzed up one of the city's most historic streets with 10 works entitled Florescer (to bloom or flourish). Look out for his trademark organic, naturalistic patterns tattooed across crumbling medieval walls.

staggering array of ports (including many fine vintage ones) and high-quality wines from the Douro, Alentejo, Dão and beyond. Prices are reasonable and it's possible to arrange a tasting and shipping. (www.garrafeiracarmo.com; Rua do Carmo 17; ⏰9am-7pm Mon-Fri, to 1pm Sat)

Armazém
CRAFTS, VINTAGE

34 🔒 MAP P86, B7

Bang on trend with Porto's current thirst for creative spaces is the hipsterish Armazém, located in a converted warehouse down by the river. A gallery, cafe and store all under one roof, with an open fire burning at its centre, it sells a pinch of everything – vintage garb, antiques, vinyl, artwork, ceramics and funky Portuguese-designed bags and fashion. (Rua da Miragaia 93; ⏰11.30am-8pm)

Explore ◈
Vila Nova de Gaia

Vila Nova de Gaia wings you back to the 17th-century beginnings of port-wine production, when British merchants transformed wine into the postdinner tipple of choice by adding a dash of brandy. Their grand lodges sit imposingly astride the Douro, inviting you for tours of barrel-lined cellars, tastings, and dinner at rooftop terraces with twinkling views of the historic centre opposite.

Trot across Ponte de Dom Luís I for far-reaching views of the city and Rio Douro below. You'll emerge at the palm-speckled Jardim do Morro (p99). From here, ride the Teleférico de Gaia (p100) down to the riverfront.

Get versed in port wine at Espaço Porto Cruz (p99), offering exhibitions and tastings, followed by lunch with a view at De Castro Gaia (p104). Next up: port lodges. Top billing for city views, informative cellar tours and tastings goes to rivals Graham's (p100) and Taylor's (p100).

As the last sun creeps across Ribeira's facades, sip an aperitif at 360º Terrace Lounge (p106), before dinner at super-stylish, hilltop Vinum (p105).

Getting There & Around
Ⓜ **Metro** Line D runs through the Jardim do Morro stop.

⛴ **Ferry** The **Douro River Taxi** (☏223 742 800; www.dourorivertaxi.com; Av Diogo Leite; one-way fare €3; ⏱10am-sunset) runs from Cais da Estiva in Porto's Ribeira district to Vila Nova de Gaia waterfront.

Vila Nova de Gaia Map on p98

Wine-tasting hall, Taylor's (p100) HERACLES KRITIKOS / SHUTTERSTOCK ©

Vila Nova de Gaia

Rio Douro

Ponte de Dom Luís I

Douro Azul 9

Graham's

5

19

R Rei Ramiro

Ferreira 14

Av Ramos Pinto

Barcadouro

Ramos Pinto

Mercado Beira-Rio 13

R Guilherme Gomes Fernandes

R Dom Afonso III

R Serpa Pinto

Turismo Espaço (Gaia) Porto 16

Espaço Porto Cruz 2

23

22

7

Kopke

Cálem 8

R Barroca

Sandeman 17 11

ReFun GPS Tours 10

R França 21

Largo Santa Marinha

Croft 12

Av Manoel de Oliveira

R Barão de Forrester

Taylor's 6

R do Choupelo

R Cândido dos Reis

20

18

Av Diogo Leite

15

Teleférico de Gaia

Calçada Serra 4

Jardim do Morro 1

Jardim do Morro

R Pilar

R Gen Torres

R Rocha Leão

Mosteiro da Serra do Pilar 3

Jardim do Morro

Av República

R Gen Torres

General Torres

N

200 m
0.1 miles

Sights

Jardim do Morro GARDENS

1 ◉ MAP P98, F2

The cable car swings up to this hilltop park, which can also be reached by crossing the upper level of Ponte de Dom Luís I. Shaded by palms, these gardens are all about the view. From here, Porto is reduced to postcard format, with the pastel-hued houses of Ribeira on the opposite side of the Douro and the snaking river below. (Av da República)

Espaço Porto Cruz WINERY, MUSEUM

2 ◉ MAP P98, D2

This swanky port-wine emporium inside a restored 18th-century riverside building celebrates all things port. In addition to a shop where tastings are held (by the glass starting at €3 or €9.50 for three ports), there's a rooftop terrace with panoramic views and 3rd-floor De Castro Gaia (p104) restaurant. The 1st and 2nd floors are given over to a small, free, port-related exhibition, the highlight of which is the 360-degree wine journey – a virtual flight over Porto and the Douro. (www.myportocruz.com; Largo Miguel Bombarda 23; ◷ 11am-7pm Tue-Sun)

Mosteiro da Serra do Pilar MONASTERY

3 ◉ MAP P98, F2

Watching over Gaia is this 17th-century hilltop monastery, with its striking circular cloister, church

Mosteiro da Serra do Pilar

SEAN PAVONE / SHUTTERSTOCK ©

with gilded altar, and stellar river views from its cupola (it's one of the few places where you can glimpse the Ponte de Dom Luís I from above). Requisitioned by the future Duke of Wellington during the Peninsular War (1807–14), it still belongs to the Portuguese military. (Rampa do Infante Santo; adult/child €4/2; ⏰10am-6.30pm Tue-Sun Apr-Oct, to 5.30pm Nov-Mar)

Teleférico de Gaia   CABLE CAR

4 ◉ MAP P98, E2

Don't miss a ride on the Teleférico de Gaia, an aerial gondola that provides fine views over the Douro and Porto on its short, five-minute jaunt. It runs between the southern end of the Ponte de Dom Luís I and the riverside. (www.gaiacablecar.com; one way/return €6/9; ⏰10am-8pm May-Sep, to 6pm Oct-Mar)

Graham's   WINE

5 ◉ MAP P98, A1

One of the original British-founded Gaia wine cellars, established way back in 1820, Graham's has been totally revamped and now features a small museum. It's a big name and a popular choice for tours, which last around 30 minutes, dip into atmospheric barrel-lined cellars and conclude with a tasting of three to eight port wines (tour prices vary according to quality). (☎223 776 492, 223 776 490; grahams@grahamsportlodge.com; Rua do Agro 141; tours incl tasting from €15; ⏰9.30am-6pm Apr-Oct, to 5.30pm Nov-Mar)

Taylor's   WINE

6 ◉ MAP P98, C4

Up from the river, British-run Taylor's boasts lovely, oh-so-English grounds with tremendous views of Porto. Its audioguide tours, available in eight languages, include a tasting of two top-of-the-range port wines (Chip Dry White and Late Bottled Vintage) – your reward for the short huff uphill. (☎223 742 800; www.taylor.pt; Rua do Choupelo 250; tours incl tasting adult/child €15/6; ⏰10am-6pm)

Sandeman   WINE

7 ◉ MAP P98, D2

Housed in an imposing granite building, Sandeman is a perfect first port of call for those who are new to port. It's free to visit the museum, showcasing port-related paintings and memorabilia whisking you back to 1790 when the young Scotsman George Sandeman started dabbling in the port and sherry trade. Guides dressed in black capes and hats lead the tours. (☎223 740 533; www.sandeman.com; Largo Miguel Bombarda 3; museum free, guided tours incl tasting €12-40; ⏰10am-8pm Mar-Oct, 10am-12.30pm & 2-6pm Nov-Feb)

Cálem   WINE

8 ◉ MAP P98, E2

Making port since 1859, these award-winning wine cellars are among Porto's most attractive. Available in several languages, the informative, entertaining guided

Port-Wine Primer

It was probably the wine-quaffing Romans who planted the first vines in the Douro Valley some 2000 years ago, but tradition credits the discovery of port itself to 17th-century British merchants. With their own country doing feisty battle with the French, they turned to their old ally Portugal to meet their wine-drinking needs. The Douro Valley was a particularly productive area, though its wines were dark and astringent. According to legend, the British threw in some brandy with the grape juice, both to take off the wine's bite, pep it up a bit and preserve it for shipment back to England and – hey presto! – port wine was born. Truth be told, the method may have already been used in the region, though what is certain is that the Brits took to the stuff with a vengeance. They built the grand lodges that speckle the hillside in Vila Nova de Gaia, a testament to their new favourite tipple, and they refined the art of making it – a fact still evidenced by some of port's most illustrious names, including Taylor's, Graham's, Sandeman and Ramos Pinto.

Port-wine grapes are born out of adversity. The vines march up the steep, rocky terraces of the Douro with little water or even much soil, and their roots must reach down as far as 30m, past layers of acidic schist (shale-like stone) to find nourishment. Vines endure extreme heat in summer and freezing temperatures in winter – the ideal conditions to stand up to the infusions. The most common grape varieties are hardy, dark reds such as *touriga*, *tinto cão* and *tinto barroca*.

Grapes are harvested by hand in autumn and are immediately crushed (often still by foot, the best way to extract aromas and produce wines with balance, structure and depth of flavour). They are allowed to ferment until alcohol levels reach 7%. At this point, one part brandy is added to every four parts wine. Fermentation stops immediately, leaving the unfermented sugars that make port sweet. The quality of grapes, together with the ways the wine is aged and stored, determines the kind of port you get.

tours last around 30 minutes and include a video screening in one of the huge oak vats used for port ageing. A visit concludes with a tasting of two port wines – usually a ruby and a white. (📞 916 113 451; www.calem.pt; Av Diogo Leite 344;

tours incl tasting €12; ⏰10am-7pm May-Oct, to 6pm Nov-Apr)

Douro Azul BOATING

9 ◉ MAP P98, A1

Douro Azul is the largest of several outfits that offer cruises in ersatz *barcos rabelos,* the colourful boats that were once used to transport port wine from the vineyards. Cruises last 45 to 55 minutes and depart at least hourly on summer days. Board at Cais de Gaia. Audioguides are available in 16 languages. (☏223 402 500; www.douroazul.com; Cais de Gaia; 6-bridges cruise adult/child €12/6; ☺9.30am-6pm)

eFun GPS Tours   TOURS

10 ◉ MAP P98, D2

Whether you want to explore Porto on foot or head further afield by minivan, eFun GPS Tours have got it nailed. Clued-up guides lead everything from three-hour walks of the historic centre (€19) to food, port wine and olive oil tastings (€65) and Jewish heritage tours (€39), as well as excursions to Braga, Guimarães and deeper into the Douro Valley.

It also offers bike rental for €5/8/15 for two/four/24 hours. (☏220 923 270; www.efungpstours.com; Rua Cândido dos Reis 55; ☺10am-7pm)

Kopke   WINE

11 ◉ MAP P98, E2

Founded in 1638, Kopke is the oldest brand on the hill, but its lodge is not open to the public, which is why you should stop here for the smooth caramelised bite of a seriously good aged tawny. The 10-year is tasty; the 20-year is spectacular. Port-wine tastings can be matched with Arcádia

chocolates or organic olive oil. (☏223 746 660; www.sogevinus.com; Av Diogo Leite 312; tastings by the glass from €2; ☺10am-7pm May-Oct, to 6pm Nov-Apr)

Croft   WINE

12 ◉ MAP P98, C3

This grand hilltop residence houses a rustic cobbled and beamed tasting room that spills out onto a fountain-dotted terrace. Croft has been going strong since 1588. A visit to its cellars includes a tasting of three ports (a pink, a reserve and a 10-year-old tawny). (www.croftport.com; Rua Barão de Forrester 412; tours incl tasting €10; ☺10am-6pm)

Ramos Pinto   WINE

13 ◉ MAP P98, C2

Right on the riverfront, you can visit the rather grand Ramos Pinto and take a look at its historic offices and ageing cellars. The basic 40-minute tour includes a visit to the museum plus a generous five-port tasting. Tours are offered in several languages. (☏223 707 000; www.facebook.com/Ramos.Pinto.Port.Douro.Wine; Av Ramos Pinto 400; tours incl tasting €10; ☺10am-6pm May-Oct, reduced hours Nov-Apr)

Ferreira   WINE

14 ◉ MAP P98, A2

Hailing back to 1751, Ferreira is the only port-wine lodge that has been Portuguese through and through from start to finish. A classic tour of the cellars rounds out with a tasting of two ports. The most expensive tour (€40) culminates in a tasting of vintage ports. Take a peek in the *azulejos* room and museum for the low-down on the founding family. (☏ 223 746 106; https://eng.sograpevinhos.com; Av Ramos Pinto 70; tours & tastings €12-40; ☺10am-6pm Mar-Oct, 10am-12.30pm & 2-6pm Nov-Feb)

Be My Guest
WALKING

To get better acquainted with Porto, sign up for one of Be My Guest's terrific themed walking tours of the city, skipping from an insider's peek at *azulejos* (hand-painted tiles) to belle époque architecture and urban art. Run by two incredibly passionate guides – Nuno and Fred – it also arranges four-hour cookery workshops (€35) and wine-tasting tours (€25). Meeting points vary. Check in advance. (☏ 938 417 850; www.bemyguestinporto.com; 3hr tours €20)

Eating

Dourum
PORTUGUESE €

15 ❌ MAP P98, E1

Matching a cosy stone-walled interior with a little pavement terrace facing the river, this bistro is literally a stone's throw from the Ponte de Dom Luís I. The friendly staff are clued up about ports and wines, which go nicely with sharing boards of Portuguese cheeses and hams, and traditional mains. (☏ 220 917 911; www.dourum.pt; Av

By the River

The covered food market **Mercado Beira-Rio** (Map p98, C2; www.mercadobeirario.pt; Av Ramos Pinto 148; ☺10am-midnight Sun-Wed, to 2am Thu-Sat) is a very welcome addition to Gaia's riverfront. Nip in and see what takes your fancy at the independently run food stalls – there's everything here from gourmet sandwiches to roast suckling pig, cheese platters, desserts and ice cream, not to mention a decent wine and port selection. The communal tables are humming come lunchtime.

Diogo Leite 454; mains €8.50-14.50; ☺noon-11pm)

Gelateria Porto Cruz
ICE CREAM €

16 ❌ MAP P98, D2

Port-flavoured ice cream...what's not to love? This modish new gelateria is the perfect pit stop for a hot day – grab a cone and head down to the riverfront to watch the world drift on by. (Av Diogo Leite 154; ice cream €2.50-4.50; ☺12.30-8pm Tue-Sun; ♿)

Taberninha Do Manel
PORTUGUESE €€

17 ❌ MAP P98, E2

Super-friendly service, big views across the Douro to Ribeira, and

Port Varieties & Food Pairing

Ruby Aged at least two years in vats; ruby hues and sweet, full-bodied fruity flavours. Goes nicely with cheese and chocolate desserts.

White Made from white port grapes and aged for two to three years; served chilled. Mixed with tonic water, it makes a refreshing summer aperitif.

Tawny Aged for two to seven years in oak casks; mahogany colours, mellow and nutty, with butterscotchy flavours.

Aged tawny Selected from higher-quality grapes, then aged for many years in wooden casks; subtler and silkier than regular tawny. Great as an aperitif or with fruit-based desserts, cheeses and pâtés.

Vintage Made from the finest grapes from a single outstanding year. Aged in vats for two years, then in bottles for at least 10 years. Sophisticated and extremely complex. Enjoy with strong blue cheeses.

Late-bottled vintage (LBV) Made from very select grapes of a single year, aged for around five years in wooden casks, then bottled; similar to vintage but ready for immediate drinking once bottled, and usually lighter bodied.

a menu crammed with well-executed Portuguese classics – Iberian pork, *petiscos* (tapas), *bacalhau* (dried-salt cold) in different guises – reel folk into Taberninha Do Manel. There's pavement seating for warm days and a rustic interior jam-packed with what looks like the contents of your grandmother's attic. (223 753 549; www.taberninhadomanel.comportugal.com; Av Diogo Leite 308; mains €11-18; 11am-midnight Tue-Sun)

De Castro Gaia INTERNATIONAL €€

Polished concrete, slatted wood and clean lines give this restaurant in the Espaço Porto Cruz (see 2 ⊙

Map p98, D2) a slick, contemporary look. The menu matches reasonably priced ports and wines with *petiscos* and mains such as octopus rice and pork cheeks cooked in red wine and cumin. There are fine views across the Douro to the houses of old Porto spilling down the hillside. (910 553 559; www.myportocruz.com; Largo Miguel Bombarda 23, Espaço Porto Cruz; petiscos €5-10, mains €10-16.50; 12.30-3pm & 7.30-11pm Tue-Sat, 12.30-3pm Sun)

Yeatman GASTRONOMY €€€

18 MAP P98, D4

With its polished service, elegant setting and dazzling views over river and city, the Michelin-starred restaurant at the five-star Yeatman Hotel is sheer class. Chef Ricardo Costa puts his imaginative spin on seasonal ingredients from lobster to pheasant – all skilfully cooked, served with flair and expertly matched with wines from the 1000-bottle cellar that is among the country's best. (📞 220 133 100; www.the-yeatman-hotel.com; Rua do Choupelo 88, Yeatman Hotel; tasting menus €140-160, wine pairing €60-70; ⏲ 7.30-11pm)

Vinum PORTUGUESE €€€

19 🗺 MAP P98, A1

Vinum manages the delicate act of combining 19th-century port-lodge charm with contemporary edge. Peer through to the barrel-lined cellar from the pine-beamed restaurant, or out across the Douro and Porto's rooftops from the conservatory and terrace. Portuguese menu stunners include green ceviche fresh from Matasinhos fish market and dry-aged Trás-os-Montes beef, complemented by a stellar selection of wines and ports. (📞 220 930 417; www.vinumatgrahams.com; Rua do Agro 141, Graham's Port Lodge; mains €18-29, menus €50-90; ⏲ 12.30-4pm & 7-11pm)

Blini GASTRONOMY €€€

20 🗺 MAP P98, E3

Overseen by Portuguese star chef José Cordeiro, the Blini is a chic newcomer to Gaia. The reflective cube perches atop a historic town house, its wraparound glass walls affording astonishing views

Vinum

M. SOBREIRA / ALAMY STOCK PHOTO ©

of historic Porto. You might begin with caviar-topped blinis, followed by stunning seafood options, from fresh oysters with lemon butter and samphire to octopus baked in red wine with turnip purée. (📞224 055 306; http://theblini.com; Rua do General Torres 344; menus €60-90; 🕐5pm-midnight Mon, noon-3pm & 5pm-midnight Tue-Sat)

Drinking

7G Roaster
COFFEE

21 🚇 MAP P98, D2

The baristas really know their stuff at this speciality coffee roasters. In the cool, monochrome, wood-floored space, you can sip a perfectly made espresso or go for brunch (€12), which includes everything from sheep's cheese to homemade granola, pastries and fresh-pressed juice. Sit on the terrace to gaze up at the vertical garden. (www.facebook.com/7groaster; Rua de França 26; 🕐10am-7pm)

360° Terrace Lounge
WINE BAR

From its perch atop the Espaço Porto Cruz (see 2 ◉ Map p98, D2), this decked terrace affords expansive views over both sides of the Douro and the city, fading into a hazy distance where the river meets the sea. As day softens into dusk, this is a prime sunset spot for sipping a glass of port or a cocktail while drinking in the incredible vista. (www.myportocruz.com; Largo Miguel Bombarda 23, Espaço Porto

Cruz; 🕐12.30pm-12.30am Tue-Thu, to 1.30am Fri & Sat, to 7pm Sun)

Esplanada do Teleférico
BAR

From its hilltop perch just above the Teleférico (see 4 ◉ Map p98, E2), this glass-fronted bar makes the most of the sensational views of Ponte de Dom Luís I and Ribeira across the river. It's a chilled spot for a coffee, beer or snack (€2.50 to €8). Sunset is naturally prime-time viewing. (www.facebook.com/esplanadateleferico; Rua Rocha Leão; 🕐10am-7pm)

Dick's Bar
WINE BAR

With a private-member's-club feel, Dick's is a class act at the Yeatman (see 18 ◉ Map p98, D4), with plush sofas for conversing, live music between 9.30pm and midnight from Thursday to Saturday, and access to one of Portugal's best cellars. Head onto the terrace to sip a glass of vintage tawny or Douro red as historic Porto starts to twinkle on the opposite side of the river. (www.the-yeatman-hotel.com; Rua do Choupelo 88, Yeatman Hotel; 🕐9am-1am Sun-Thu, to 2.30am Fri & Sat)

Entertainment

Fado in Porto
FADO

Lisbon and Coimbra may be the spiritual home of fado, Portugal's unique brand of melancholic folk music with guitar accompaniment, but you'll find decent performances over a glass of port or two at the Cálem cellars (see 8 ◉ Map p98,

Gaia's Lodges

Since the mid-18th century, port-wine bottlers and exporters have been obliged to maintain their 'lodges' – basically dressed-up warehouses – here in Vila Nova de Gaia. Today some 60 of them clamber up the steep riverbank, and at night the entire scene turns into Portugal's version of Las Vegas, with huge neon signs clamouring for the attention of winos and oenophiles alike.

This enclave of historic terracotta-topped warehouses is now Porto's best-known attraction, despite not actually being in the city at all; Vila Nova de Gaia is a wholly separate municipality, and – beyond the riverbank – goes about its own business in a kind of parallel universe.

About two dozen lodges are open for tours and tastings on weekdays and Saturday. In high season (June to September), the larger ones run visitors through like clockwork and you'll wait no more than 15 minutes to join a tour. At other times they can accommodate you more or less on the spot.

E2) most evenings. (☎223 746 660; http://fadoinporto.com; Av Diogo Leite 344; cover €21; ⏱6.30pm Tue-Sun Apr-Oct, 6pm Tue-Sun Nov-Mar)

Shopping

Porto Wine House   FOOD & DRINKS

22 🔒 MAP P98, D2

Stock up on fine whites, rubies and tawnies here, as well as *conservas* (tinned fish), preserves and other goodies. Ships worldwide. (www.portowinehouse.com; Rua Cândido dos Reis 4-10; ⏱9am-8pm)

Casa do Galo   GIFTS & SOUVENIRS

23 🔒 MAP P98, D2

An ode to all things Portuguese, this shop is well stocked with gifts from the kitsch to the classy. You'll find *galo de Barcelos* cockerels, as well as ceramics, textiles (lace and *lenços dos namorado,* or sweetheart handkerchiefs), cork products and edibles such as honey, preserves, tinned fish in retro wrappings and, naturally, port wine. (www.acasadogalo.com; Av Diogo Leite 50; ⏱10.30am-8.30pm)

Top Sight 📷

Afurada

Sitting pretty on the banks of the Douro, this breezy fishing village has remained charmingly oblivious to 21st-century trends. Even getting here on the creaking wooden boat crossing the river is like time travel. Afurada is in high spirits in summer, when it hosts two must-see festivals – Festa de São Pedro da Afurada (in late June) and MEO Marés Vivas (http://maresvivas. meo.pt, in late July).

Getting There

⚓ Local boats make the quick hop across the Douro, departing from Cais do Ouro (near the Ponte da Arrábida) every 15 minutes from 7am to 9pm. A one-way ticket costs €1.50.

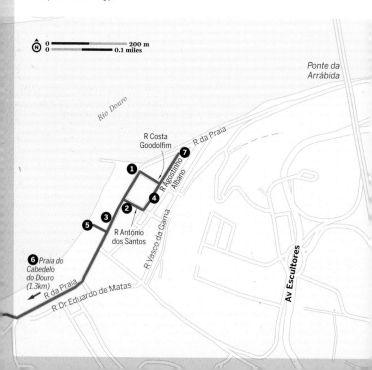

❶ River Stroll

The lure of the sea is tangible here, with squawking gulls wheeling in the sky, washing strung out to dry in the briny breezes, and fishers tending to their nets and preparing their tackle. Stroll the **waterfront** to see a delightfully untouristy side to Porto and enjoy broad views – Foz across the water and the hazy smudge of the Atlantic on the horizon.

❷ Market Mornings

Get up early to catch the small but lively fish market, **Mercado da Afurada** (Rua da Praia), in full swing. The fishers sell cod, sardines and other Atlantic catches amid tangled nets and in rapid-fire Portuguese.

❸ Public Laundry

Washing machines are installed in every house, but local *donas* (ladies) still swear by the daily ritual of stone washtubs and good old-fashioned elbow grease at the **lavadouro público** (Public Laundry; Rua da Praia). A blast from a bygone age, this is where they come to wash their whites, natter and sing – a social gathering with abundant soaping and scrubbing.

❹ Fish Lunch

Fado drifts up the *azulejo* (hand-painted tile) walls, toddlers tear through the dining room and plump, oily sardines (and other fresh fish) are roasted on sidewalk grills at **Taberna São Pedro** (📞912 477 659, 986 732 466; Rua Costa Goodofilm 84; mains €10-15; ⏱10am-4pm & 7-11pm Mon-Sat, 10am-4pm Sun). There's much to love in this forever-packed seafood house, one block inland from the ferry pier.

❺ Stylish Marina

Architects Barbosa & Guimaraes have left their imprint on the **Douro Marina** (www.douromarina.com; Rua da Praia; ⏱8.30am-8pm) complex, a vision in glass and steel with forms that mirror the shapes of boat masts and sails. It has a sailing academy, shops and cafes, and a bike-rental place.

❻ Beach Breezes

Nothing blows away the city cobwebs like a wander along **Praia do Cabedelo do Douro**, fringed by the protected dunes of the Douro Estuary Nature Reserve. It's a relaxed spot to kick back on the sand and watch the gentle rise and fall of the Atlantic – especially as sunset pinkens the sky.

❼ Dinner with a View

Back in Afurada, go for dinner at riverfront **A Margem** (📞227 724 788; Rua Agostinho Albano 18; mains €19-26; ⏱11am-3pm & 7-10pm Mon-Sat, 11am-3pm Sun), with astounding views of the Ponte da Arrábida through its floor-to-ceiling glass windows. This is a popular choice for its winningly fresh seafood.

Explore

Massarelos

Low-key Massarelos snuggles alongside Miragaia on the riverfront. If you want to slip off the well-trodden trail, this neighbourhood of breezy views and niche museums will appeal. Slow the pace with a languid stroll in Porto's most fetching garden or spend time in one of the interesting museums in the neighbourhood.

Take a bracing walk along the river, stopping to glimpse the 18th-century Igreja do Corpo Santo de Massarelos (p117). Weave uphill for a stroll in the Jardins do Palácio de Cristal (p112), where botanical species thrive and miradouros (viewpoints) command sensational city views. Next up is the Museu Român-tico (p117), once home to an exiled Sardinian king.

After a simple lunch at Taberna Cais das Pedras (p118), visit the Museu do Carro Eléctrico (p118), with its fine stash of vintage trams, or dare to scale the Ponte da Arrábida (p117) with Porto Bridge Climb (p118).

As day fades, go for sundowners at chilled roof terrace Miradouro Ignez (p120).

Getting There & Around

Tram Vintage tram 1 (Infante–Passeio Alegre) stops in Massarelos en route between the historic centre and Foz do Douro.

Bus Useful buses include line 200 (Bolhão–Foz) and 201 (Aliados–Viso), both stopping at Jardins do Palácio de Cristal. Night bus 1M from Aliados serves Massarelos.

Massarelos Map on p116

Ponte da Arrábida (p117) KPZFOTO / ALAMY STOCK PHOTO ©

Top Sight

Jardins do Palácio de Cristal

Sitting atop a bluff, this gorgeous botanical garden is one of Porto's best-loved escapes, with lawns interwoven with sun-dappled paths, dotted with fountains and sculptures, and bristling with giant magnolias, camellias, cypresses and olive trees. It's actually a mosaic of small gardens that open up little by little as you wander – as do the arresting views.

◉ **MAP P116, D2**

Rua Dom Manuel II

🕙 8am-9pm Apr-Sep, to 7pm Oct-Mar

🚻

Gardens

Laid out in the 19th century by German landscape architect Émille David, the gardens attract everyone from couples to families, joggers and photographers. There are pockets of woodland and picnic areas, as well as rose and aromatic herb, hedge and parterre gardens to explore. The Jardim dos Sentimentos (Garden of Feelings) hides the beautiful *Dor* bronze by sculptor António Teixeira Lopes.

Miradouros

On the park's southern fringes are viewpoints that grant front-row views of the city. You'll see the Ponte de Dom Luís I loping across the sparkling Rio Douro, the historic centre, and the port lodges cascading down the hillside in Vila Nova de Gaia.

Museu Romântico

On the south slopes is the small but stately home where the exiled king of Sardinia spent his final days in 1843. It has been turned into a museum (p117) featuring the king's belongings, oil paintings and period furnishings displayed in elegant salons.

Avenida das Tílias

The sunlight streams through the lime trees that proudly line this avenue – use it as a central reference point to get your bearings.

Pavilhão Rosa Mota

This striking domed pavilion was built to replace the original Palácio de Cristal (Crystal Palace) in 1956. It harbours a multi-media library, auditorium and cafe, and hosts sport events, exhibitions, theatre and musical performances.

★ Top Tips

o The gardens are at their loveliest in early spring when everything is in bloom.

o Come at sunset to see the sky blush pink above Porto and watch the port lodges on the opposite side of the river light up.

o Visit the Museu Romântico at the weekend for free entry.

✕ Take a Break

Open when the gardens are, the kiosk is a laid-back spot for a drink and you might spot the odd passing peacock.

Go gourmet with an outstanding lunch at nearby Michelin-starred restaurant Antiqvvm (p120).

Walking Tour 🥾

Exploring Rua Miguel Bombarda

Porto is abuzz with new-found energy and emerging creativity on and around graffiti-splashed Rua Miguel Bombarda. A nose around its galleries, boutiques and cafes reveals the city from a more urban, edgy angle. If you want to plug into the artistic groove of 21st-century Porto, this is where it's at.

Walk Facts

Start Galeria São Mamede

End Capela Incomum

Length 900m; a couple of hours depending on your stops

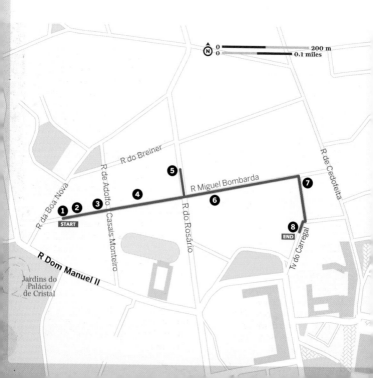

❶ Gallery Hop

Mooch around the cluster of galleries at the western end of Rua Miguel Bombarda. Top billing goes to **Galeria São Mamede** (www.saomamede.com; ⏰ 2-8pm Tue-Fri, 3-8pm Sat), at No. 624. The gallery hosts rotating exhibitions, such as the recent one spotlighting the works of contemporary Portuguese sculptor Paulo Neves. You might want to also take a peek in at No. 570, Galeria Presença (www.galeriapresenca.pt; ⏰ 10am-12.30pm & 3-7pm Mon-Fri, 3-7pm Sat), which homes in on both home-grown and international modern art.

❷ Arty Burgers

Creativity in these parts extends to the grill at **BUGO** (📞 226 062 179; www.bugo.com.pt; burgers €8-13.50; ⏰ noon-3pm & 7.30-11pm Mon-Thu, noon-3pm & 7.30pm-midnight Fri, noon-4pm & 7.30pm-midnight Sat) at No. 598. It's an upbeat nosh spot for gourmet burgers from veggie to Black Angus varieties. A satisfying lunch here will set you back just €10.

❸ Portuguese Creatives

A showcase for established and emerging Portuguese artists, **Galeria Fernando Santos** (www.galeriafernandosantos.com; ⏰ 3-7.30pm Mon & Sat, 10am-12.30pm & 3-7.30pm Tue-Fri) at No. 526, brings contemporary art to the fore. In the past it has featured the abstract sculpture of Pedro Valdez Cardoso and the paintings of much-lauded Pedro Cabrita Reis. One of the first galleries on Rua Miguel Bombarda, it's still among the best.

❹ Folk Art Finds

A relative newcomer to Porto's art scene at No. 452, **Cruzes Canhoto** (📞 223 197 406; www.cruzescanhoto.com; ⏰ 10am-8pm) places the accent on primitive and folk art. Many of the paintings and sculptures bear the hallmark of self-taught artists, and much is for sale.

❺ Boutique Buys

Indie boutique-cum-gallery **CRU** (www.cru-cowork.com; Rua do Rosário 211; ⏰ 10am-8pm Mon-Fri, 2-8pm Sat) is a shop window for innovative Portuguese designers and artists, for everything from fashion and footwear to ceramics and accessories.

❻ Modish Mall

Among the galleries along Rua Miguel Bombarda, at No. 285 is the unique, independent shopping mall **CC Bombarda** (⏰ noon-8pm Mon-Sat), where you'll find stores selling locally designed urban wear, organic cosmetics, jewellery, vinyl and other hipster-pleasing delights.

❼ Art of Illustration

Round out your gallery-hop with the art of illustration (mostly Portuguese, some international) at No. 61 **Ó! Galeria** (www.ogaleria.com; ⏰ noon-8pm Mon-Sat). Prints range from geometric patterns to wackier pieces. It does a nice selection of T-shirts, books and postcards.

❽ High Spirits

Where better to revive your spirits than over a glass of Douro red at chapel-turned-trendy-bar **Capela Incomum** (p92).

Massarelos

Porto Bridge Climb

R do Rosário

R Alberto A Gouveia

R do Breiner

R de Miguel Bombarda

R de Adolfo Casais Monteiro

R da Boa Nova

R Dom Manuel II

R Jorge de Viterbo Ferreira

R da Restauração

Largo da Alfândega

World of Discoveries

R de Miragaia

R Nova da Alfândega

R Armazéns

Look at Porto

Praça da Galiza

R da Piedade

R de Vilar

Jardins do Palácio de Cristal

R de Quintães

5 Museu Romântico

MASSARELOS

R Fonte de Massarelos

R da Restauração

R de Monchique

R do Bicalho

R Dom Pedro V

R dos Moinhos

Museu do Carro Eléctrico

Alameda Basílio Teles

Porto Sky Experience 7

Igreja do Corpo Santo de Massarelos

Cais das Pedras

R de Ouro

Rio Douro

Ponte da Arrábida

For reviews see

◎	Top Sights	p112
◉	Sights	p117
✕	Eating	p118
🍸	Drinking	p120
🛍	Shopping	p121

400 m
0.2 miles

Sights

Ponte da Arrábida BRIDGE

1 ⊙ MAP P116, A2

Arcing 270m in a single swoop over the Douro River and linking Porto to Vila Nova de Gaia, this mighty bridge is visible from afar. Designed by prominent Portuguese civil engineer Edgar Cardoso, it was the world's longest concrete bridge at the time of its completion in 1963. Climb (p118) it if you dare for knockout views of the river and city.

Igreja do Corpo Santo de Massarelos CHURCH

2 ⊙ MAP P116, B3

Rising above the riverfront with a facade adorned in blue-and-white *azulejos* (hand-painted tiles), this church was built in 1776 on the site of a chapel that was founded by the Confraria das Almas do Corpo Santo de Massarelos in 1394. Prince Henry the Navigator once belonged to this brotherhood of mariners and the great explorer appears on a tiled panel. (Church of the Holy Body of Massarelos; Largo do Adro; ⊙7-8pm Tue, 3-8pm Sat)

Look at Porto THEATRE

3 ⊙ MAP P116, F4

This new 5D cinema whisks you on a virtual flight over Porto, revealing angles never seen at ground level, with added special effects such as motion seats, water spray and different aromas bringing the city to life. It's a fun sensory attraction and a sure-fire winner with kids. (www.lookatporto.pt; Rua da Atafona/ Rua da Ancira 6-8; adult/child €8/6; ⊙10am-8pm Mar-Oct, to 7pm Nov-Feb; ⚹)

World of Discoveries AMUSEMENT PARK

4 ⊙ MAP P116, E4

A guaranteed kid-pleaser – if slightly overpriced – this interactive museum catapults you back to the 14th to 16th centuries, when the Portuguese ruled the colonial waves. The latest technological wizardry and a swashbuckling, theme-park-like boat ride recreate scenes of the intrepid seafarers of yore. (www.worldofdiscoveries.com; Rua de Miragaia 106; adult/child €14/8; ⊙10am-6pm Mon-Fri, to 7pm Sat & Sun; ⚹)

Museu Romântico MUSEUM

5 ⊙ MAP P116, C2

Nestled on the southern slopes of Jardins do Palácio de Cristal, beneath cathedral oaks and sycamores, is the small but stately home where the exiled king of Sardinia spent his final days holed up in 1843. Reopened in 2018 following extensive renovation, the house has been turned into an appealing museum featuring the king's belongings and dainty period furnishings displayed in elegant salons. (Quinta da Macieirinha; Rua de Entre Quintas 220; adult/child weekdays €2.20/free, Sat & Sun free; ⊙10am-5.30pm Tue-Sun)

Porto Bridge Climb

Porto has some cracking bridges, and while the Ponte de Dom Luís I is most famous (you know, that one built Eiffel Tower–style), the Arrábida Bridge is also a marvel and was the world's largest concrete arch bridge when it was completed in 1963. So if you fancy a view with a thrill, you can harness up and **climb** (Map p116, A2; ✆ 929 207 117; www.portobridgeclimb.com; Rua do Ouro 680; adults from €12.50; ◷2.15pm-sunset) the 65m structure.

Museu do Carro Eléctrico   MUSEUM

6 ◉ MAP P116, B2

Housed in an antiquated switching-house, this museum is a tram-spotter's delight. It displays dozens of beautifully restored old trams – from early 1870s models once pulled by mules to streamlined, bee-yellow 1930s numbers. (Tram Museum; www.museudocarroelectrico. pt; Alameda Basílio Teles 51; adult/child €8/4; ◷2-6pm Mon, 10am-6pm Tue-Sun)

Porto Sky Experience   SCENIC FLIGHTS

7 ◉ MAP P116, B3

If you fancy seeing Porto's tangled streets and awe-inspiring river with a bird's-eye view, book yourself a 10-, 15- or 20-minute slot on the Helitour chopper. You'll whiz past key attractions such as the Torre dos Clérigos, Ponte de Dom Luís I and Porto's beaches, before gracefully twirling your way down onto the over-river helipad. (Porto & Douro Experiences – Helitours; ✆ 225 432 464; www.portoandlisbon.pt/ porto/helitours; Alameda Basílio Teles; from €150; ◷9am-1pm & 2.30-6pm)

Eating

Taberna Cais das Pedras   PORTUGUESE €

8 ✖ MAP P116, C3

A warm, homely vision of chequered tablecloths and wood floors, this tavern rustles up an appetising assortment of *petiscos* (small plates), such as clams, flame-grilled *chouriço*, *pataniscas* (fish fritters) and *feijoada* (pork and bean casserole) – all for pocket-money prices. Sharing is the way to go. (✆913 164 584; Rua Monchique 65; petiscos €2.50-5; ◷2pm-2am Tue-Sun)

Casa d'Oro   PIZZA €

9 ✖ MAP P116, A2

For pop-up views of the Ponte da Arrábida illuminated, you can't beat this concrete-and-glass clay-oven pizzeria leaning over the Douro. It rustles up terrific pizzas including *diavola* (spicy salami and oregano), *Vesuvio* (sausage and broccoli) and *fichi e prosciutto* (prosciutto and fig). (✆226 106 012; Rua do Ouro 797; pizzas €8-14; ◷12.30-3pm & 8-11pm Mon-Thu, 12.30pm-midnight Fri-Sun)

Caseirinho   PORTUGUESE €

A real locals' haunt, Caseirinho (see 2 ⊙ Map p116, B3) is a genuine, great-value pick. Dishes are authentically Portuguese, along the lines of *arroz de marisco* (rice and seafood stew), freshly cooked fish and *tripas à moda do Porto* (Porto-style tripe with white bean stew). You might have to wait, but the food is worth it. (📞226 066 222; Cais das Pedras 40; lunch €7.50, mains €5-12; ⊙noon-3pm & 7-10pm Mon-Sat)

O Antigo Carteiro   PORTUGUESE €€

10 ✕ MAP P116, A2

Coyly tucked away on a lane back from the river, O Antigo Carteiro is as close as you'll get to eating in a Portuguese family home. Attentive, clued-up staff pair regional wines with well-executed classics – garlicky octopus, pork tenderloin, *bacalhau com broa* (codfish with cornbread crust) and the like. (📞937 317 523; www.facebook.com/oantigocarteiro; Rua Senhor da Boa Morte 55; mains €14-19; ⊙noon-11pm Tue-Sat; 👬)

Papavinhos   PORTUGUESE €€

11 ✕ MAP P116, D4

This no-frills, family-run tavern extends a warm welcome and dishes up generous portions of home-cooking. Try for a window table to see the river twinkle at night as you dig into classics such as clams in garlic and *bacalhau com broa* (codfish with cornbread bread) with a glass of crisp house white.

(📞222 000 204; Rua de Monchique 23; mains €10-27.50; ⊙noon-3pm & 7-11pm Tue-Sun)

33 Alameda   MEDITERRANEAN €€

12 ✕ MAP P116, B3

Housed in the old Bolsa do Pescado fish market, now the stylish hotel **Vincci Porto** (📞220 439 620; https://en.vincciporto.com; Alameda de Basílio Teles 29; d €106-253, tr €151-296, ste €156-288; P 📶), this high-ceilinged, strikingly lit restaurant is an atmospheric backdrop for Portuguese and Mediterranean cuisine with a twist. Starters such as *alheira* (Portuguese sausage) with pepper ice cream prelude well-executed mains including coriander-crusted hake with tomato *açorda* (stew). The three-course €11 lunch menu is a steal. (📞220 439 620; mains €14-18; ⊙12.30-3pm & 7.30-11pm)

Gull   JAPANESE, SUSHI €€

13 ✕ MAP P116, C3

This slinky sushi lounge opens onto a decked terrace overlooking the Douro, or you can retreat to the softly lit, wood-floored interior, with bold art gracing white walls. The resident chef keeps the super-fresh sushi and ceviche coming, and the mood gets clubbier as day spills into night. (📞914 300 038; www.gull.pt; Cais das Pedras 15; sushi lunch €13-16, sushi sets €19-65; ⊙noon-3pm & 8-11pm Mon-Thu, noon-3pm & 8pm-midnight Fri, 1-4pm & 8pm-midnight Sat, 1-4pm & 8-11pm Sun)

The Sausage with a Story

Found on many a restaurant menu in Porto, the beloved *alheira* sausage is cheap, filling comfort food, whether boiled and served with cabbage and potatoes or – as is more commonly the case – fried and dished up with a runny egg and fries. Taking its name from the Portuguese word for garlic (*alho*), which is often an ingredient, it's a smoky, tangy number, well seasoned with paprika and with an almost pâté-like consistency.

The sausage has a fascinating history. It was first created by the Jewish population during the Portuguese Inquisition (1536–1821), when Jews were forced to convert to Christianity. Jews could easily be spotted by the fact that they didn't hang sausages in the *fumeiros* (smokehouses), so they came up with a cunning plan to fool the Inquisition by inventing a delicious nonpork sausage. The *alheira*, originally a mix of chicken, duck, rabbit, venison, quail or veal and bread, was born. While many versions of the *alheira* now contain pork, you'll still find some that don't.

Monchique   PORTUGUESE €€

14 MAP P116, C3

Down by the river, this restaurant morphs into a bar as the night wears on. Stone arches, art-slung walls and candlelight create a cosy vibe for *petiscos,* seafood and traditional Portuguese mains. There's often live music at the weekends, skipping from fado to jazz. (926 714 127; www.facebook.com/monchique.barconcerto; Cais das Pedras 5; petiscos €2-9.50, mains €7.50-15; 7.30pm-2am)

Antiqvvm   GASTRONOMY €€€

15 MAP P116, C2

What a delight this tucked-away Michelin-starred restaurant is, ensconced in the revamped stone arcades of 19th-century Quinta da Macieirinha. Vítor Matos heads up the kitchen, serving ingredient-driven dishes – truffle and Wagyu beef, and sea bass with algae and Azores saffron – with flair and artistry. With entrancing views out over Porto from the garden terrace, this is one for special occasions. (226 000 445, 912 024 754; http://antiqvvm.pt; Rua de Entre Quintas 220; menus €25-120; noon-midnight Tue-Sat, noon-3pm Sun)

Drinking

Miradouro Ignez   ROOFTOP BAR

16 MAP P116, D3

This relatively new roof terrace has swiftly become one of the hippest hang-outs in Massarelos, with knockout views of the river and Vila Nova de Gaia across the water.

Traditional sausage dish

It's a chilled place for a smoothie or sundowner. (www.facebook.com/miradouroignez; Rua da Restauração 252; ⊘10am-midnight Mon-Thu, 10am-2am Fri & Sat, 10am-9pm Sun)

Shopping

Monseo
JEWELLERY

17 🔒 MAP P116, A2

If you're looking for unique, Portuguese-designed jewellery, you'll find just that at this strikingly lit boutique. Many of the pieces are embedded with gemstones or emblazoned with Portuguese motifs. (www.monseo.com; Rua do Ouro 120; ⊘10.30am-1.30pm & 3-7pm Mon-Fri)

Kubik Gallery
ART

18 🔒 MAP P116, B3

Click into the local arts scene by stopping by this contemporary gallery, which showcases the work of established and up-and-coming Portuguese and international artists in its rotating exhibitions. (www.kubikgallery.com; Rua da Restauração 6; ⊘3-7.30pm Tue-Sat)

NATALIA MYLOVA / SHUTTERSTOCK ©

Explore ⊕
Boavista

The city's longest avenue, Avenida da Boavista, blazes through Boavista, with its rooftop bars, urbane hotels and landmarks designed by Pritzker Prize–winning duo Álvaro Siza Vieira and Eduardo Souto de Moura. Beyond the postmodern Casa da Música concert hall, you'll find less touristed (if heavily trafficked) streets that are home to botanical gardens and a synagogue.

No building has more pulling power in Porto than the Casa da Música (p124), a futuristic Rem Koolhaas number. Join a tour of the avant-garde interior. Traffic whizzes around the monument-topped Jardim da Boavista (p128) opposite, while the nearby Mercado Bom Sucesso (p130) food market throngs with hungry tripeiros (Porto residents). Join them here or head to the Urban Cicle Café (p128) for a creative brunch.

Swinging west brings you to Sinagoga Kadoorie (p127), Portugal's biggest synagogue, and the lake-speckled Jardim Botânico do Porto (p127).

In the evening, return to catch a concert at the Casa da Música (p133) and a view from its rooftop bar (p132).

Getting There & Around

M Metro Five out of Porto's six metro lines stop at Casa da Música, centrally positioned for exploring the neighbourhood.

🚌 Bus Handy buses include line 200 (Bolhão–Foz), 201 (Aliados–Viso) running through Boavista, riverfront line 500 (Praça Liberdade–Matosinhos) and line 502 (Bolhão–Matosinhos), which runs the entire length of Avenida da Boavista.

Boavista Map on p126

Mercado Bom Sucesso (p130) JEFF GREENBERG / CONTRIBUTOR / GETTY IMAGES ©

Top Sight 📷
Casa da Música

All at once minimalist, iconic and daringly imaginative, the Casa da Música is the beating heart of Porto's cultural scene and home to the Porto National Orchestra. Dutch architect Rem Koolhaas rocked the musical world with this crystalline creation – the jewel in the European Capital of Culture 2001 crown. The behemoth conceals a shoebox-style concert hall muchlauded for its acoustics.

◉ **MAP P126, D2**

📞 220 120 220

www.casadamusica.com

Avenida da Boavista
604-610

guided tour €10

🕑 English guided tours
11am & 4pm

Striking Architecture

The Casa da Música is a scene-stealer. Harmonious and grand from a distance, its perspectives distort as you approach its facade. Shaped like an irregular polygon, this rough diamond of a building looks as though it has been teleported from another time and place. Carpeted in pinkish-gold travertine marble, the plaza buzzes with skateboarders swooping across its undulations.

Acoustic Marvel

An architectural sensation, the 1300-seat main auditorium, Sala Suggia, uses Nordic plywood, double-curved glass walls and chairs specially adapted to improve acoustics. The hall's name pays tribute to the famous Porto cellist, Guilhermina Suggia (1885–1950). Gold leaf runs through the walls like grain through wood, and it's the only concert hall in the world lit exclusively with natural light – daytime concerts here are special.

Tile Traditions

Rem Koolhaas interplays the links between Portugal and Holland in the striking VIP Room clad with *azeulejos* (hand-painted tiles). Adorning one wall are blue-and-white *azulejo* panels replicating those at São Bento train station, depicting the 1415 conquest of Ceuta and national greats like Henry the Navigator. In a nod to his homeland, the other wall is embellished with Delft-style motifs.

Renaissance Room

It's all an optical illusion in this quirky room, patterned with geometric 3D tiles that deliberately throw you off-centre. These cubic tiles reflect Renaissance styles, which played on perspective – these again rose to popularity in the works of the Op Art movement in the 1960s.

★ Top Tips

o There's only one ticket price per concert as fantastic acoustics mean there is not a bad seat in the house.

o Be sure to visit the terrace – on clear days you can see the distant fizz of the Atlantic.

o English-speaking guided tours at 11am and 4pm daily cost €10, last around an hour and give you a great insight into the building.

✕ Take a Break

Step up to Restaurant Casa da Música (p130) for swoon-worthy city views and Mediterranean food with a twist.

It's a quick hop to the Dog (p128) for gourmet *cachorros* (hot dogs) between sightseeing.

Boavista

500 m
0.25 miles

R da Quinta Amarela

Carolina Michaelis Ⓜ

R de Oliveira Monteiro

R António Pedroso de Fátima

R de Nossa Senhora de Fátima

Praça de Pedro Nunes

R de J Vasconcelos

R do Pedro Cruz

Av da França

Casa da Música Ⓜ

Jardim da Boavista ◉4

R Júlio Dinis

Praça da Galiza

Casa da Música ◎

Praça de Mouzinho de Albuquerque

Mercado Bom Sucesso ◉15

R do Bom Sucesso ✕12

R de 5 de Outubro

R Gonçalo Sampaio

◉17

R Campo Alegre

✕9 ◐16 ◐10 ◐8

R de Agramonte

Cemitério de Agramonte ◎1

R de João de Deus

R Monsenhor Fonseca Soares

Av da Boavista

Pedro Hispano

R Tenente Valadim

R de António Patrício

R de Feliciano de Castilho

R Guerra Junqueiro

Sinagoga Kadoorie ◉2

R Soares de Passos

R Guilherme Braga

R Campo Alegre

✕11 ▲

◐13

R de António Cardoso

Foz do Douro (3.3km)

Jardim Botânico do Porto ◉3

★14

Sights

Cemitério de Agramonte   CEMETERY

1 ◉ MAP P126, C3

Opened in 1855 to bury the victims of a cholera epidemic, today the Agramonte Cemetery is one of Porto's most beautiful cemeteries The city's wealthiest residents bankrolled its monuments and exuberant mausoleums, some of which are adorned with sculptures by Soares dos Reis and Teixeira Lopes. The cemetery is particularly appealing in spring when the camellias and magnolias are in bloom. (Rua de Agramonte; ◷8.30am-5pm)

Sinagoga Kadoorie   SYNAGOGUE

2 ◉ MAP P126, B3

Sidling up to the Cemitério de Agramonte, the Kadoorie Synagogue is the largest in the Iberian Peninsula and a visible reminder of the importance of the city's Jewish community. It was inaugurated in 1938. For a peek of the beautifully tiled interior and an insight into the workings of the synagogue, hook onto a guided visit of the museum. (www.comunidade-israelita-porto.org; Rua Guerra Junqueiro 340; adult/child €5/2; ◷2-5.30pm Sun-Fri)

Jardim Botânico do Porto   GARDENS

3 ◉ MAP P126, A4

Run by the Faculty of Sciences of Porto University, this jigsaw of

Cemitério de Agramonte

ELIAS GARRIDO / SHUTTERSTOCK ©

botanical gardens is a cool escape on hot summer days. Dotted with lakes and flourishing with succulents, roses and camellias, these secluded gardens are the brainchild of port-wine merchant João Henrique Andresen, who had them laid out in romantic style in 1895. (https://jardimbotanico.up.pt; Rua do Campo Alegre 1191; admission free; ⏱9am-5pm Mon-Fri, 10am-6pm Sat & Sun)

Jardim da Boavista

GARDENS

4 📍 MAP P126, D3

A park at the centre of one of Porto's busiest roundabouts, the Jardim da Boavista provides shade and respite from the hustle and bustle of the city. Its centrepiece is the *Monumento aos Heróis da Guerra Peninsular* (Monument to the Heroes of the Peninsular War) that commemorates the Portuguese and British victory over Napoleon's troops in the Peninsular War (1808–14). (Praça de Mouzinho de Albuquerque; admission free)

Eating

Urban Cicle Café

CAFE €

5 🍴 MAP P126, D3

A hip hang-out in central Boavista, this cycle cafe has bikes dangling from the ceiling and terrific brunches (€14) until 3pm, with omelettes, homemade cakes and tarts, Greek yoghurt with granola – the works. (📞220 981 308; www.easy-cicle.pt; Praça do Bom Sucesso 18;

snacks & light mains €3-8; ⏱8.30am-8pm Mon-Fri, 10am-8pm Sat; 📶)

Ponto Dois

CAFE €

6 🍴 MAP P126, D2

Join the white-collar crowd from Porto's financial district for a quick lunch or pastry in this sleek and modern cafe. There's plenty of room for everyone to pack into the industrial-style interior, or bag yourself a table on the patio out the back to catch a ray of sunshine. (📞919 257 911; www.facebook.com/ponto2porto; Av de França 202; toasts from €2.50; ⏱7.30am-7.30pm Mon-Thu, to 8pm Fri, 8am-8pm Sat; 📶)

Dog

FAST FOOD €

7 🍴 MAP P126, D2

No clues here for guessing that the house speciality is *cachorros* (hot dogs), albeit with gourmet toppings like brie and honey and onions cooked in port wine. Take a perch at the bar at this hip new haunt just steps from the Casa da Música. (📞220 144 433; Rua de 5 de Outubro 111; hot dogs €3.50-5; ⏱noon-11pm Mon-Sat)

Casinha Boutique Café

CAFE €

8 🍴 MAP P126, C2

All pretty pastel shades and hidden garden alcoves, this cafe lodged in a restored 19th-century town house is a sweet deal, despite the rather indifferent service. Wholesome, locally sourced ingredients go into freshly prepared sand-

Porto's Architectural Heavyweights

Porto has become a city to watch on the global architecture scene. Many of the city's newest landmarks are striking in their simplicity and carefully choreographed to blend in with the natural surrounds. Two architects in particular have been instrumental in changing the face of the city.

One is Pritzker Prize winner and Portuguese starchitect **Álvaro Siza Vieira**. Born in Matasinhos in 1933, he has designed dozens of buildings and public spaces all over the city – from the minimalist, angular Museu de Arte Contemporânea to the clean, crisp aesthetic of the clifftop Boa Nova Tea House. He has left his imprint on housing projects and office blocks around Avenida da Boavista, the glazed tiles and granite of São Bento metro station, and the Piscinas das Mares in Matasinhos, saltwater swimming pools that snuggle into the rocky seafront. Underpinning all of his designs is a lightness and fluidity of form that echoes his desire for continuity in architecture, and his belief that nothing exists in isolation.

Another Porto-born hero and fellow Pritzker Prize winner is **Eduardo Souto de Moura**, who was taken under the wing of Álvaro Siza Vieira as a budding architect before opening his own practice in 1980. Like his mentor, Souto de Moura has poured his talent into public projects – from revamping metro stations (Casa da Música, Trindade, Aliados and Bolhão included) to the Casa das Artes cultural centre where he finds expression in natural materials and purity of form. Among his other standouts are the Burgo Tower, with the dual character of its facade – juxtaposing horizontal with vertical, opaque with transparent. More playful still is his space-age Casa do Cinema Manoel da Oliveira in Foz, a futuristically modernist edifice with protruding windows.

The dream duo finely tuned their act before exporting it overseas, collaborating on numerous projects together – from London's curvaceous, latticework Serpentine Gallery Pavilion in 2005 to the Sensing Spaces exhibition at the Royal Academy in 2014. For a self-guided tour of their Porto creations, pick up the free architecture maps and guides at the tourist office.

wiches, quiches, salads, crepes and desserts. There's also a deli for takeaway Portuguese olive oils, wines, preserves and more. (☏934 021 001; www.casinhaboutique.com; Av da Boavista 854; mains €4.50-12; ◷9am-midnight Mon-Sat, 10am-10pm Sun; ☎)

To Market, To Market!

Foodies are in their element in the **Mercado Bom Sucesso** (Map p126, D3; www.mercadobomsucesso.pt; Praça Bom Sucesso; ⏰10am-11pm Sun-Thu, to midnight Fri & Sat) food court, which is perfect grazing territory with stands selling everything from fresh sushi to piadina (Italian flat-bread sandwiches), tapas, ice cream and Portuguese sparkling wine. The Traveller Café is a good pit stop for freshly pressed juices and smoothies or coffee and pastries. If you're looking for edible gifts to take home, stop by Sabores e Tradição, which stocks gourmet products from the Trás-os-Montes, such as cheese, olive oil and honey.

The fresh produce market does a brisk trade in fish and shellfish, meat, fruit and vegetables and flowers from 10am to 8pm Monday to Saturday.

Essência
VEGETARIAN €€

9 MAP P126, C1

This bright, modern brasserie is famous Porto-wide for its generous vegetarian (and nonvegetarian!) dishes, stretching from wholesome soups and salads to curries, pasta dishes, risotto and *feijoada* (pork and bean casserole). There's a terrace for warm-weather dining. (☏228 301 813; www.essencia restaurantevegetariano.com; Rua de Pedro Hispano 1190; mains €10.50-15; ⏰12.30-3pm & 8-10.30pm Mon-Thu, to midnight Fri & Sat; 🖥️)

Restaurante Casa da Música
INTERNATIONAL €€

This restaurant on the 7th floor of the Casa da Música (see ◉ Map p126, D2) opens onto a black-and-white tiled terrace granting superlative views of the cityscape. Clever back-lit art and lofty ceilings create a slick, urban backdrop for bright and simple Med-inspired flavours, such as octopus carpaccio with herb salad and parmesan tuile or sea bass with mussel stew and lemon zest. (House of Music; ☏220 107 160; www.casadamusica.com; Av da Boavista 604; mains €16.50-18.50, lunch/dinner menu €14.50/19.50; ⏰12.30-3pm & 7.30-11pm Mon-Thu, to midnight Fri & Sat; 🛜🖥️)

Em Carne Viva
VEGETARIAN €€

10 MAP P126, C2

An elegant stucco-adorned parlour and a romantic garden set the scene for creative takes on vegetarian and vegan dishes – including the *francesinha* reinterpreted to chunky bean burgers with fries – all served on beautiful crockery. Save room for the scrumptious desserts. (☏932 352 722, 220 925 598; www.emcarneviva.pt; Av da Boavista 868; 2-course menu €9.50, mains €11-20;

noon-3pm & 7.30-10pm Mon-Thu, 12.30-3.30pm & 7-11pm Sat; 🖋)

Casa do Bu

CAFE €€

11 🗺 MAP P126, A1

Stone walls, clean lines and a funky modern fireplace create a contemporary look at this new urban cafe. Tank up on vitamins with a freshly made juice or salad, or opt for *petiscos* (Portuguese-style tapas). Lunch (soup plus the day's special) is good value at €7.50. (Rua Eugénio de Castro 97; petiscos €4-7, mains €14-17; ⏰7am-8pm; 📶)

Casa Agrícola

PORTUGUESE €€€

12 🗺 MAP P126, D4

Abutting a chapel, this beautifully restored, 18th-century rural house is a splash of historic charm in an otherwise modern neighbourhood. The 1st-floor restaurant exudes old-world sophistication, with its polished-wood floor, bistro seating and chandeliers. It's an intimate choice for Portuguese flavours such as monkfish *cataplana* (stew). The more informal cafe-bar downstairs has a happy hour from 4pm to 8pm. (📞226 053 350; www.casa-agricola.com; Rua do Bom Sucesso 241; mains €17-29; ⏰12.30-3pm & 8-10.30pm Mon-Sat)

Porto Novo

INTERNATIONAL €€€

13 🗺 MAP P126, A2

One for special occasions, this refined, modern restaurant in the Sheraton sets the scene with high-back caramel chairs, pristine white tablecloths and ceramic lights. The vibe is sophisticated, the service

Scone dish, Em Carne Viva (p130)

EMILY MCAULIFFE / LONELY PLANET ©

Boavista Eating

---

attentive and the menu skips from suckling pig in orange sauce and wood-oven roasted codfish in an olive crust to spot-on pizza. The three-course €22 lunch offers good value. (📞 220 404 000; www.portonovorestaurante.com; Rua Tenente Valadim 146, Sheraton Porto Hotel & Spa; mains €24-39; ⏱12.30-3pm & 8-11pm Mon-Fri, 1-3pm & 8-11.30pm Sat & Sun; 👬)

Drinking

Bar Casa da Música   BAR

Situated on the top floor of Porto's most strikingly contemporary building, Casa da Música (see ◎ Map p126, D2), this bar is a fine place to sip a drink as the city starts to light up – the terrace commands great views. DJs occasionally work the decks at the twice-monthly Saturday clubbing sessions (11pm to 4am). See the website for more details. (House of Music; www.casadamusica.com; Av da Boavista 604; ⏱12.30-3pm & 7.30-11pm Mon-Thu, to midnight Fri & Sat; 🔊)

New Yorker Bar   BAR

This upscale, contemporary bar at the Sheraton (see 13 ✖ Map p126, A2) is a sophisticated – if pricey – choice for coffee, cocktails and conversing. Head to the garden terrace when the weather is warm. (www.sheratonporto.com; Rua Tenente Valadim 146, Sheraton Porto Hotel & Spa; ⏱10am-1am Sun-Thu, to 1.30am Fri & Sat)

Bar Casa da Música

HANS GEORG ROTH / GETTY IMAGES ©

Entertainment

Casa da Música   CONCERT VENUE

Grand and minimalist, sophisticated yet populist, Porto's cultural behemoth (see Map p126, D2) boasts a shoebox-style concert hall at its heart, meticulously engineered to accommodate everything from jazz duets to Beethoven's Ninth. (House of Music; ☎220 120 220; www.casadamusica.com; Av da Boavista 604; ⌚box office 9.30am-7pm Mon-Sat, to 6pm Sun)

Boavista FC   FOOTBALL

14 ⭐ MAP P126, A1

FC Porto's worthy cross-town rival, Boavista FC's home turf is the Estádio do Bessa, which lies just off Avenida da Boavista. Check the local editions of *Jornal de Notícias* for upcoming matches. (www.boavistafc.pt; Rua 1° de Janeiro, Estádio do Bessa Século)

Shopping

Pura Filigrana   JEWELLERY

15 🅰 MAP P126, D3

Housed in the Mercado Bom Sucesso, this little pop-up is a showcase for dainty Portuguese filigree jewellery, from classic styles to contemporary slants. (www.facebook.com/pg/PURA.Filigree; Mercado Bom Sucesso, Praça Bom Sucesso; ⌚10am-11pm Sun-Thu, to midnight Fri & Sat)

Nuno Baltazar   FASHION & ACCESSORIES

16 🅰 MAP P126, C2

This is the flagship of designer Nuno Baltazar, Portugal's king of the catwalk. Pop in to take a look at his latest collections, which are always urbanely elegant and beautifully cut. (☎226 054 982; www.nunobaltazar.com; Av da Boavista 856; ⌚10.30am-1.30pm & 2.30-7.30pm Tue-Sat)

Península Boutique Center   MALL

17 🅰 MAP P126, D3

This modern mall harbours a range of Portuguese and international brands, with a focus on fashion and labels such as Massimo Dutti, Adolfo Dominguez, Bimba y Lola and Purificación García, as well as a handful of jewellers, a perfumery and a cafe, Ponto K. (www.peninsula.pt; Praça Bom Sucesso 159; ⌚10am-10pm Mon-Sat, to 8pm Sun; 📶)

Explore ◎
Foz do Douro
& Around

Out west, Foz do Douro dances to its own relaxed beat, with beach bars humming with bronzed locals, lighthouses commanding big ocean views, botanical gardens for strolling, and one of Porto's two Michelin-starred restaurants. Wander the esplanade to the backbeat of the Atlantic and kick back on the beach with an ice cream. Board tram 1 for a ride along the riverfront from Ribeira to the pretty gardens of Jardim do Passeio Alegre (p139).

The Atlantic crashes against the landmark Farol Senhora da Luz (p139) lighthouse. From here, wander along the esplanade, pausing for drinks at beach bar Praia da Luz (p140). Mosey north to Matosinhos, pausing for an alfresco fish lunch on grill-lined Rua Heróis de França.

Return to Foz for a shady stroll in the vast Parque da Cidade (p143). For dinner, book a table at seafront stunner Boa Nova Tea House (p143) or Michelin-starred Pedro Lemos (p140). Finish with a beer at shipshape Bonaparte (p140).

Getting There & Around

🚋 **Tram** Tram 1 (Infante–Passeio Alegre) trundles between the historic centre and Foz do Douro.

🚌 **Bus** Bus 500, which runs from central stops in Porto such as Praça da Liberdade and Ribeira (Infante), makes several stops in Foz en route to Matosinhos.

Foz do Douro Map on p138

Farol Senhora da Luz (p139) ANASTASIA PETROVA / SHUTTERSTOCK ©

Top Sight 📷
Serralves

One of Porto's blockbuster cultural attractions, Serralves, combining a museum, mansion and extensive gardens, is just off the Avenida da Boavista that powers west from Boavista to Foz. Bearing the indelible imprint of Porto starchitect Álvaro Siza Vieira, the gallery wows with a stellar permanent collection from the late 1960s to the present day as well as rotating exhibitions. The fountain- and sculpture-dotted gardens revive museum-weary eyes.

◎ MAP P138, D3

www.serralves.pt

Rua Dom João de Castro 210

adult/child museums & park €10/free, park only €5/free

🕙10am-7pm Mon-Fri, to 8pm Sat & Sun May-Sep, reduced hours Oct-Mar

Álvaro Siza Vieira Architecture

Local architecture demigod Álvaro Siza Vieira seized the reins to design the Museu de Arte Contemporânea in 1991, making an intuitive transition between the gallery and its grounds. His two-winged, U-shaped, bleached-white edifice reveals clean geometric forms and precise lines. With skylights and windows framing the landscape to 'bring it inside', the Pritzker Prize–winning architect's creation is all at once voluminous, luminous and fluid.

Contemporary Art

Zooming in on contemporary art from the 1960s to the present day, the museum's enticing roster of rotating exhibitions is in tune with prevailing artistic currents and draws a line between eminent and emerging Portuguese and international artists. These skip from boundary-pushing thematic exhibitions to retrospectives.

Art Deco Villa

Casa de Serralves is one of Portugal's most formidable exponents of art deco architecture. Inspired by his travels in Paris, Carlos Alberto Cabral, the second Count of Vizela, had the villa built in Streamline Moderne style between 1925 and 1944, embellishing its interiors with neoclassical finesse. He enlisted the eminent architects and artists of the age, including René Lalique (skylight) and Alfred Porteneuve (powder-puff pink facade).

Garden Strolls

Serralves' 18-hectare park forges a link between art and the natural world. Designed by French landscape architect Jacques Gréber in the 1930s, its a harmonious ensemble of parterres, beech and oak groves, tree-lined avenues and camellia and rose gardens. Keep an eye out for outdoor art, such as Claes Oldenburg's giant shovel *Plantoir* (2001).

★ Top Tips

o Free entry from 10am to 1pm on the first Sunday of the month.

o Browse the website for a clickable park map.

o For total cultural immersion, time your visit for the free and fabulous Serralves em Festa in early June.

✕ Take a Break

Head to the museum **restaurant** (✆ 226 170 355; Rua Dom João de Castro 21; lunch buffet €13; ◷ noon-7pm Mon-Fri, 10am-7pm Sat, to 8pm Sun) for a lunch buffet or to the teahouse terrace for a drink.

Hop on a bus for the five-minute ride to Foz for a light lunch with Atlantic views at seafront Tavi (p139).

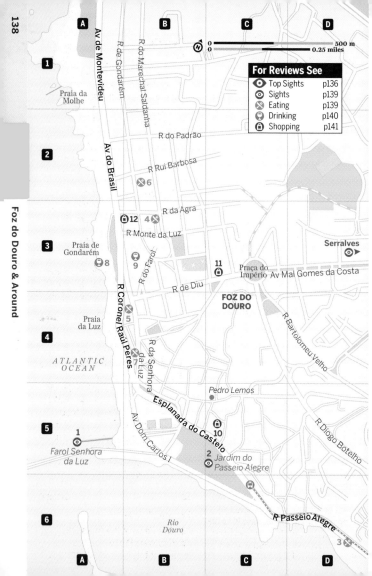

For Reviews See

◉	Top Sights	p136
◎	Sights	p139
⊗	Eating	p139
🍷	Drinking	p140
🛍	Shopping	p141

0 — 500 m
0 — 0.25 miles

Av de Montevideu

R de Gondarém

R do Marechal Saldanha

R do Padrão

Av do Brasil

R Rui Barbosa

⊗ 6

🛍 12 4 ⊗

R da Agra

R Monte da Luz

Praia de Gondarém

🍷 8

Serralves
◎ ►

🍷 9

R do Farol

11 🛍

Praça do Império Av Mal Gomes da Costa

R de Diu

FOZ DO DOURO

Praia da Molhe

ATLANTIC OCEAN

Praia da Luz

R Coronel Raúl Peres

⊗ 5

R da Senhora da Luz

R Bartolomeu Velho

Pedro Lemos ●

Esplanada do Castelo

Av Dom Carlos I

🛍 10

2 ◎ Jardim do Passeio Alegre

R Diogo Botelho

1 ◉
Farol Senhora da Luz

Rio Douro

R Passeio Alegre

3 ⊗

Sights

Farol Senhora da Luz   LIGHTHOUSE

1 ⊙ MAP P138, A5

One of Foz do Douro's most visible icons, this lighthouse stands on an esplanade, bearing the full brunt of the swells and storms of the Atlantic. Take a bracing stroll here for big, mind-stilling views of ocean and sky. (Av Dom Carlos I)

Jardim do Passeio Alegre   GARDENS

2 ⊙ MAP P138, C5

A joy for the aimless ambler, this 19th-century garden is flanked by graceful old buildings and dotted with willowy palms, sculptures, fountains and a bandstand that occasionally stages concerts in summer. Listen to the crash of the ocean as you wander its tree-canopied avenues. There's also crazy golf for the kids. (Rua Passeio Alegre; ♦)

Eating

Mercearia do Miguel   CAFE €

3 🍴 MAP P138, D6

A bright, retro-cool cafe in a born-again 1950s grocery store by the seafront, the Mercearia do Miguel is a wholly inviting choice for a healthy breakfast (try the açai bowl with homemade granola), a detox juice, great coffee and cake, or lunches ranging from gourmet salads to bruschetti, sandwiches and *petiscos* (tapas). Head for the patio when the sun's out. (📞 220 116 889; www.

Beach Life

Foz has a trio of decent (if rocky) beaches, great for a paddle. Fringed by an esplanade, generously sized Praia da Luz nudges up to Praia de Gondarém, a slim strip of sand that disappears at high tide, which in turn sidles up to the wider Praia da Molhe. This is where locals come to unplug, so the beaches are often crammed on summer weekends; come on weekdays in low season and you'll have them pretty much to yourself.

merceariadomiguel.com; Rua do Passeio Alegre 130; snacks €3-4.50, petiscos €1-9; ⊙ 9.30am-6.30pm Wed-Sun; 🍴 ♦)

Bird   CAFE €

4 🍴 MAP P138, B3

With its vintage birdcage lanterns, pretty floral prints and foliage-draped patio, this cafe is as cute as a button. It's a wonderfully relaxed spot for lunch (a soup, main and drink goes for a wallet-friendly €8.50), a slice of cake and tea, or brunch. There's ample choice for vegetarians, too. (Rua da Agra 143; lunch €8.50, brunch €12, petiscos €3-8; ⊙ 11am-7pm Mon-Thu, to 8pm Fri-Sun; 🍴)

Tavi   SWEETS €

5 🍴 MAP P138, B4

Alluring views of the thrashing Atlantic draw Porto locals to the terrace of this renowned seafront

Gourmet Highs

One of Porto's two Michelin-starred restaurants, **Pedro Lemos** (Map p138, C5; 220 115 986; www.pedrolemos.net; Rua do Padre Luís Cabral 974; tasting menus €100-120; 12.30-3pm & 7.30-11pm Tue-Sat) is sheer delight. With a love of seasonally sourced produce and robust flavours, the eponymous chef creates culinary fireworks using first-class ingredients from land and sea – be it ultra-fresh Atlantic bivalves or Alentejano black pork cooked to smoky deliciousness with wild mushrooms. Choose between the subtly lit, cosy-chic dining room or the roof terrace.

patisserie, which has recently had a bright and breezy makeover. It rustles up light mains, creative salads and savoury crepes, but is best known for its sweet confections: chocolates, ice cream, traditional Portuguese *bolo de arroz* (rice cakes), pastries and good strong coffee. (www.confeitariatavi.com; Rua Senhora da Luz 363; sweets €2-5, mains €7-12; 8.30am-8pm)

Cafeína   MODERN EUROPEAN €€

6 MAP P138, B2

Hidden coyly away from the seafront, Cafeína has a touch of class, with soft light casting a flattering glow across its moss-green walls, crisp tablecloths, lustrous wood floors and bookcases. The food is best described as modern European, simple as stuffed squid with saffron purée or rack of lamb in a herb and lemon crust, expertly matched with Portuguese wines. (226 108 059; www.cafeina.pt; Rua do Padrão 100; 3-course lunch €18, mains €17-21; 12.30-6pm & 7.30pm-12.30am Sun-Thu, to 1.30am Fri & Sat;)

Bar Tolo   PORTUGUESE €€

7 MAP P138, B4

This fun little spot in a tall, narrow, sky-blue corner building has a tiny rooftop terrace sporting an ocean view, a rustic-chic vibe and a menu of creative *petiscos* (Portuguese-style tapas) and mains. (224 938 987; Rua da Senhora da Luz 185; mains €10-17; 12.30pm-midnight Wed-Mon)

Drinking

Praia da Luz   BAR

8 MAP P138, A3

Praia da Luz is a worthwhile stop when out exploring Porto's coastline. It rambles over tiered wooden decks to its own private rocky cove, and while you could probably skip the food, you should definitely kick back and enjoy the view over a coffee or cocktail. (www.praiadaluz.pt; Av do Brasil; 9am-2am)

Bonaparte   PUB

9 MAP P138, B3

Right on the seafront, this ship-shape pub catapults you back to the age of great maritime discoveries, with its warm, woody, lantern-lit

ISLAVICEK / SHUTTERSTOCK ©

Jardim do Passeio Alegre (p139)

interior. It's a cosy, nicely relaxed spot for a pint of Guinness. (www.bonaparteporto.net; Av do Brasil 130; ⏰5pm-2am)

Shopping

Augusto Leite FOOD

10 🔒 MAP P138, C5

Fancy packing up a picnic for the beach? You'll find the fixings you need at Augusto Leite, a delightful family-run deli, grocery store and wine shop much frequented by locals. As well as Portuguese and international cheeses, cured meats and sweets, it has excellent wood-fired bread from the Trás-os-Montes. (Rua do Passeio Alegre 924; ⏰9am-8.30pm Mon-Sat, 10.30am-1.30pm & 3.30-8pm Sun)

Mercado da Foz MARKET

11 🔒 MAP P138, C3

Stalls are piled high with fresh produce and flowers at this recently revamped covered market. There are plenty of food stands, where you can tuck into everything from Trás-os-Montes cheeses and smoked sausage to Douro wines, gourmet burgers and hot dogs, and meltingly tender *leitão* (suckling pig) from the Bairrada region. (Rua de Diu; ⏰7am-7pm Mon-Sat)

Yellow Boat FASHION & ACCESSORIES

12 🔒 MAP P138, B3

A fashion boutique, interior design and concept store rolled into one urban-cool whole. (www.theyellowboatstore.com; Av Brasil 282; ⏰2-7pm Mon, 11am-7pm Tue-Sat)

Worth a Trip 🔭
Matosinhos

Just north of the seaside suburb of Foz do Douro, Matosinhos is a genuine fishing port (and one of the best places to eat fish fresh from the Atlantic in Porto). It's a terrific day out for families and outdoorsy types, with a fort, an aquarium and Porto's biggest urban park, as well as a broad, wave-lashed beach, some striking public art and tidal swimming pools snuggled into the rocks, bearing the imprint of Portuguese architect Álvaro Siza Vieira.

Getting There

🚌 Bus 500 runs from central stops in Porto such as Praça da Liberdade and Ribeira (Infante).

Ⓜ Take the blue metro (A) to the end of the line.

Holding Fort

Also known as the Castelo do Queijo (Cheese Castle) because of the wedge of rock it stands on, **Forte de São Francisco Xavier** (Praça Gonçalves Zarco; admission €0.50; ☺1-6pm Tue-Sun; 🚹) looks like the archetypal fortress, with its sturdy ramparts, watchtowers and drawbridge. Built in 1661, it harbours a small weaponry exhibition, but more impressive is the view, especially at sunset.

Aquarium Fun

Some 5000 marine creatures splash in the tanks at **Sealife** (www.visitsealife.com; 1 Rua Particular do Castelo do Queijo; adult/child €13.50/9.50; ☺10am-6pm Mon-Fri, to 7pm Sat & Sun; 🚹), where kiddie highlights include a shark tunnel and rock pool. Aquatic oddities include glow-in-the-dark jellyfish, South American leaf fish and cow-nosed rays. The sharks are fed at 11am and 2.30pm, the rays at noon and 4pm.

Park Life

The hum of traffic soon fades as you enter the serene, green **Parque da Cidade** (Av de Boavista; 🚹) Portugal's largest urban park. Laced with 10km of walking and cycling trails, this is where locals come to unplug and recharge, picnic (especially at weekends), play ball, jog, cycle, lounge in the sun and feed the ducks on the lake.

Casting a Net

Arriving in Matosinhos, you can't help but stop dead in your tracks gazing up at *SheChanges – Anemone*, a 50m-high sculpture by North American artist Janet Echelman. The giant net, an ode to Matosinhos' fishing community, is spectacular when lit up at night. It also changes shape in the wind, hence the name.

Beach Time

A broad swathe of sand, the Praia do Matosinhos unfurls north of the fortress. You can take a dip here but be warned that the water is almost always cold! Stiff breezes and waves attract surfers and bodyboarders.

★ **Top Tips**

○ Factor in time for hanging out on the beach and strolling (or biking) the seafront promenade.

○ Matosinhos is one for fine days as most of its appeal lies outdoors.

✕ **Take a Break**

Go for a winningly fresh fish lunch on grill-lined Rua Heróis de França. The pavement terrace at **Dom Peixe** (☎ 224 927 160; www.dom peixe.com; Rua Heróis de França 241; mains €8-20; ☺noon-11pm; 🚹) is a good bet.

Splurge on a Michelin-starred lunch above the crashing Atlantic at the Álvaro Siza Vieira–designed **Boa Nova Tea House** (pictured; Casa de Cha; ☎ 229 940 066, 932 499 444; www.ruipaula. com; Av da Liberdade, Leça da Palmeira; tasting menus €90-125; ☺12.30-3pm & 7.30-11pm Tue-Sat).

Survival Guide

Barcos rabelos (boats used to transport wine) SEAN PAVONE / SHUTTERSTOCK ©

Before You Go

Book Your Stay

Websites

○ **Lonely Planet** (lonely planet.com/portugal/the-north/porto/hotels) Recommendations and bookings.

○ **Oporto Apartments** (www.oportoapartments.com) Apartment rentals in central Porto.

○ **Go Oporto** (www.gooporto.com) Lists a decent selection of hotels, hostels and centrally located apartments.

Best Budget

○ **Gallery Hostel** (www.gallery-hostel.com) Funky hostel with an arty vibe, free walking tours, and events such as port tastings.

○ **Tattva Design Hostel** (www.tattvadesignhostel.com) Super-central, on-trend backpacker digs with a rooftop lounge.

○ **Rivoli Cinema Hostel** (www.rivolicinemahostel.com) Squeaky-clean dorms with movie-themed decor.

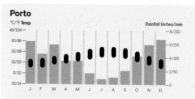

When to Go

○ **Winter** (Nov–Feb) Quiet but for specific events. Weather can be wet. Bargains abound.

○ **Spring** (Mar–May) Mild temperatures, gardens in bloom and reasonable room rates.

○ **Summer** (Jun–Aug) Peak season for open-air festivals, beach days and alfresco dining. Beds are at a premium.

○ **Autumn** (Sep & Oct) Few crowds and usually warm, though expect the odd shower.

○ **Passenger** (www.thepassengerhostel.com) Stylish hostel making tracks in Estação de São Bento.

○ **Bluesock Hostel** (www.bluesockhostels.com) Ribeira digs with a sociable vibe and historic backdrop.

○ **Gaia Porto Hostel** (www.hostelgaiaporto.pt) Sweeping river views and a warm welcome.

Best Midrange

○ **Canto de Luz** (www.cantodeluz.com) Chic little French-run guest-house with looks, personality and *magnifique* breakfasts.

○ **6 Only** (www.6only.pt) Historic meets contemporary in six super-stylish rooms.

○ **Maison Nos B&B** (www.maisonnos.com) Sweet and unique rooms with uberwelcoming hosts.

○ **Vintage Guest House** (www.portovintageguesthouse.pt) Nouveau vintage contender right in the thick of things.

○ **Casa do Conto**

(www.casadoconto.com)
A 19th-century town
house with many stories
to tell.

Best Top End

o **Yeatman** (www.the-
yeatman-hotel.com) Hilltop
stunner in Gaia, with a
spa, Michelin-starred
restaurant and port-wine
tastings.

o **ROSA ET AL Town-
house** (www.rosaetal.
pt) Classy, individually
designed suites, a lovely
garden and famous
brunches.

o **Armazém Luxury
Housing** (https://
armazemluxuryhousing.
com) A former iron
warehouse given a new
design-minded lease of
life in Ribeira's heart.

o **Torel Avantgarde**
(www.torelavantgarde.com)
Classy avant-garde five-
star hotel high on a hill in
Miragaia.

o **Pestana Porto –
A Brasileira** (www.
pestanacollection.com)
Turn-of-the-century
style in landmark
19th-century building.

o **Hotel Teatro**
(www.hotelteatro.pt)
Flamboyant design
hotel in a converted mid-
19th-century theatre.

Arriving in Porto

Francisco Sá Carneiro Airport

o **Metro** (http://
en.metrodoporto.pt) violet
line E (direction Estádio
do Dragão) links the air-
port to downtown Porto;
change at Trindade onto
yellow line D (direction
Santo Ovídio) for Aliados
and São Bento stops. A
one-way ticket costs €2
and the journey takes
around 45 minutes.

o **STCP** (Sociedade de
Transportes Colectivos
do Porto; ☎ 808 200
166; www.stcp.pt) runs a
couple of public buses
between the airport
and the centre; the
most useful is the 601
to Cordoaria, departing
every 30 minutes from
5.30am to 11.30pm. A
single costs €2.

o A daytime taxi to
central Porto costs
between €20 and €25.
The rank is just outside
the Arrivals Hall. It's
usually a 30-minute ride,
but in peak-traffic time
allow an hour or more.

São Bento Train Station

o Most *urbano, regional*
and *interregional* (IR)
trains depart from the
stunning indoor-outdoor
São Bento (Map p58,
E5; Praça Almeida Garrett)
station.

o São Bento is on the
yellow D metro line, two
stops from Aliados.

o For train timetables
and fares, visit www.
cp.pt.

Campanhã Train Station

o Porto is the principal
rail hub for northern
Portugal. Long-distance
services start at **Cam-
panhã** (Map p58, H5;

Eating Price Ranges

Prices for a main course:

Budget	€	under €10
Midrange	€€	€10–20
Top End	€€€	more than €20

Tickets & Passes

o The rechargeable **Andante Card** (www.
linhandante.com), costing €0.60 and valid for one
year, allows smooth movement between metro,
funicular, tram and many bus lines. Charge it
with the travel credit according to which zones
you will be travelling in. You can purchase credit
from metro ticket machines.

o A 24-hour pass covering the entire
network (except for the trams) costs
€4.15/5.50/6.90/8.30 for zones 2/3/4/5.

Tram, Bus & Funicular

o Porto's public trans-
port system is operated
by **STCP** (Sociedade de
Transportes Colectivos do
Porto; ☎808 200 166;
www.stcp.pt).

o Visit the website for
timetables, fares, maps
and a journey planner.

o Central hubs of Porto's
extensive bus system
include the Jardim da
Cordoaria, Praça da
Liberdade and São
Bento station.

o A one-way ticket costs
€1.95, or €1.20 with an
Andante Card.

o The panoramic
**Funicular dos
Guindais** (Map p42,
G5; one way adult/child
€2.50/1.25; ⏱8am-10pm
Sun-Thu, to midnight Fri
& Sat Apr-Oct, to 8pm
Sun-Thu, to 10pm Fri & Sat
Nov-Mar) shuttles up and
down a steep incline
from Av Gustavo Eiffel,
opposite Ponte de Dom
Luís I, to Rua Augusto
Rosa.

o Three vintage trams
trundle around the city
approximately every 30
minutes from 8am to
9pm. The most useful
line, 1E, travels along the

Rua Monte da Estação)
station, 3km east of the
centre.

o Campanhã is con-
nected to the centre by
five metro lines. It's four
stops from Trindade,
where you can change
for Aliados and São
Bento.

Getting Around

Metro

o Porto's newish
metro system (http://
en.metrodoporto.pt) is
compact and fairly easy
to navigate – though
not comprehensive.
It comprises six lines
that all converge at the

Trindade stop.

o Tickets cost
€1.20/1.60/2 for zone
2/3/4 with an Andante
Card. Zone 2 covers the
whole city centre east to
Campanhã train station,
south to Vila Nova de
Gaia and west to Foz do
Douro.

o Each trip allows you an
hour to move between
methods of transport
without additional cost.

o Tickets need to be
validated before you
begin your journey.
Wave the card in front
of a machine marked
'Andante'.

o For timetables, maps
and fares, visit the metro
website; all stations also
have maps.

o The metro runs from
around 6am to 1am.

Douro to the seaside Foz district. One-way tickets cost €3; a two-day adult/child pass costs €10/5.

Bicycle

o Despite the narrow alleyways, steep hills and cobbled streets, cyclists are ubiquitous in Porto, and there are some particularly great rides along the Douro on dedicated bike paths from Ribeira to Foz or from Vila Nova de Gaia to Afurada and beyond.

o Bike rental outlets include **Fold 'n' Visit** (Map p58, D1; ☏ 220 997 106; www.topbiketours portugal.com; Rua Alferes Malheiro 139; rental per half-/full day from €13/17), **L&L** (Map p42, B3; ☏ 223 251 722; www.lopesrenta bike.wix.com/porto; 2nd fl, Largo São Domingos 13; bike hire per 1/24hr €2.50/15; ☉10am-8pm) and **Porto Rent a Bike** (Map p42, G5; ☏ 222 022 375, 912 562 190; www.portorentabike.com; Av

Gustavo Eiffel 280; bikes per half-/full day from €10/15; ☉10am-2pm & 3-7pm). A full day's rental will set you back around €15. Many also offer guided cycling tours.

o **Vieguini** (Map p87, D8; ☏ 914 306 838; www. vieguini.pt; Rua Nova da Alfandega 7; bikes per half-/full day €8/12; ☉9am-7pm) has a great selection of high-quality mountain bikes and also rents motor scooters (€28 per day).

Taxi

o There are taxi ranks throughout the centre, or call **Táxis Invicta** (☏ 225 076 400; www. taxisinvicta.com).

o To cross town, expect to pay between €5 and €7 for daytime trips. There's a 20% surcharge at night, and an extra charge if you leave the city limits, which includes Vila Nova de Gaia.

Essential Information

Business Hours

Exceptions to the following are noted in listings:

Banks 8.30am to 3pm Monday to Friday

Bars 7pm to 2am

Cafes 9am to midnight

Nightclubs 11pm to 6am Thursday to Saturday

Post Offices 9am to 6pm Monday to Friday

Restaurants noon to 3pm & 7pm to 10pm

Shops 10am to 7pm Monday to Saturday

Discount Cards

If you intend to do a lot of sightseeing, the **Porto Card** (1-/2-/3-/4-day card €13/20/25/33) may save you money. It allows holders free or discounted admission to city museums, free travel on public transport, and discounts on cruises, tours and cultural events, as well as discounts at some restaurants and shops.

Top Tip

Many shops close on a Sunday and some shut early on Saturday. Small boutiques may close for lunch (1pm to 3pm). Monday is the day off for most museums.

The card is sold at all **Turismo do Porto** (📞300 501 920; www.visit porto.travel) tourist offices. There's also a walker's version, without public transport, which costs €6 for one day.

Electricity

Type C
230V/50Hz

Type F
230V/50Hz

Emergencies

Police, Fire & Ambulance 📞112

LGBT Travellers

Porto's gays and lesbians keep it discreet in the streets, but let their hair down in Porto's numerous gay-friendly night spots. Most venues are clustered around Jardim da Cordoaria. Gay Pride festivities take place in the first or second weekend in July. Consult www. portugalgay.pt for listings, events and other information.

Money

○ The Portuguese currency is the euro (€), divided into 100 cents.

○ Visa is widely accepted, as is MasterCard; American Express and Diners less so, with the exception of top-end hotels and restaurants.

○ Multibanco ATMs are widespread (look for the MB logo). Your home bank will usually charge around 1% to 2% per transaction.

○ There is a currency exchange, open from 7am to 8pm, as well as several 24-hour ATMs, in the airport arrivals hall.

○ Service is not usually added to the bill. Tip an average of 10% for decent service in restaurants. It's courteous to leave a bit of spare change in bars and cafes. Round up to the nearest euro in taxis.

Public Holidays

Banks, offices, department stores and some shops close on the public holidays listed.

New Year's Day 1 January

Carnaval Tuesday February/March; the day before Ash Wednesday

Good Friday March/April

Liberty Day 25 April

Labour Day 1 May

Corpus Christi May/June; ninth Thursday after Easter

Portugal Day 10 June; also known as Camões and Communities Day

Feast of the Assumption 15 August

Republic Day 5 October

All Saints' Day
1 November

Independence Day
1 December

Feast of the Immaculate Conception
8 December

Christmas Day
25 December

Safe Travel

Porto is generally a very safe city with a low crime rate.

o Keep an eye on your valuables on the city's trams and metro, where pickpockets and bag-snatchers occasionally operate, especially in rush-hour crowds, as well as at other tourist hubs such as Rua das Flores and Cais da Ribeira.

o Be wary of your surroundings at night in the alleys of Ribeira district as well as in the area between the cathedral and São Bento train station.

Toilets

o Public toilets in Porto are few and far between, but you'll often find public toilets at train and major metro stations, as well as in department stores and malls.

o Your best bet is to pop into the nearest cafe or bar. If you just want to use the loo, order a *cimbalinho* (espresso) – one of the cheapest things on the menu.

Tourist Information

City Centre Turismo (Map p58, D2; ☎ 300 501 920; www.visitporto.travel; Rua Clube dos Fenianos 25; ☺ 9am-8pm May-Oct, to 7pm Nov-Apr, to 9pm Aug) The main city turismo has a detailed city map, a transport map and the Agenda do Porto cultural calendar, among other printed materials.

iPoint Campanhã (Map p58, H6; www.visitporto.travel; Estação de Comboio de Campanhã; ☺ 9.30am-6.30pm Jun-Aug) Seasonal information point run by the *turismo* at the Campanhã train station

iPoint Ribeira (Map p42, D6; www.visitporto.travel; Praça da Ribeira; ☺ 10am-7pm Apr-Oct) Useful *turismo*-run information point on Praça da Ribeira, open seasonally.

Turismo (Gaia) (Map p98, D2; ☎ 223 758 288; www.cm-gaia.pt; Av Diogo Leite 135; ☺ 10am-6pm Mon-Sat) Gaia's *turismo* dispenses a good town map and a brochure listing all the lodges open for tours.

Turismo (Sé) (Map p42, E4; ☎ 300 501 920; www.visitporto.travel; Terreiro da Sé; ☺ 9am-8pm May-Oct, to 7pm Nov-Apr) Handy tourist office right next to the cathedral. Offers a ticket and hotel booking service.

Top Tip

Bear in mind that some small, family-run shops, guesthouses and restaurants accept cash only – if in doubt, ask first.

Language

Most sounds in Portuguese are also found in English. The exceptions are the nasal vowels (represented in our pronunciation guides by '*ng*' after the vowel), pronounced as if you're trying to make the sound through your nose; and the strongly rolled *r* (represented by '*rr*' in our pronunciation guides). The symbol '*zh*' sounds like the 's' in 'pleasure'. Keeping these points in mind and reading the pronunciation guides as if they were English, you'll be understood just fine. The stressed syllables are indicated with italics. To enhance your trip with a phrasebook, visit lonelyplanet.com. Lonely Planet iPhone phrasebooks are available through the Apple App store.

Basics

Hello.
Olá.   o·*laa*

Goodbye.
Adeus.   a·de·*oosh*

How are you?
Como está?   ko·moo *shtaa*

Fine, and you?
Bem, e você?   beng e vo·*se*

Please.
Por favor.   poor fa·*vor*

Thank you.
Obrigado. (m)   o·bree·*gaa*·doo
Obrigada. (f)   o·bree·*gaa*·da

Excuse me.
Faz favor.   faash fa·*vor*

Sorry.
Desculpe.   desh·*kool*·pe

Yes./No.
Sim./Não.   seeng/nowng

I don't understand.
Não entendo.   nowng eng·*teng*·doo

Do you speak English?
Fala inglês?   faa·la eeng·*glesh*

Eating & Drinking

..., please.   *..., por favor.*   ..., poor fa·*vor*

A coffee   *Um café*   oong ka·*fe*

A table   *Uma mesa*   oo·ma me·za
for two   *para duas*   pa·ra oo·ash
                pessoas   pe·so·ash

Two
beers   *Dois*   doysh
                cervejas   ser·*ve*·zhash

I'm a vegetarian.
Eu sou   e·oo soh
vegetariano/   ve·zhe·a·ree·a·noo/
vegetariana. (m/f) ve·zhe·a·ree·a·na

Cheers!
Saúde!   sa·*oo*·de

That was delicious!
Isto estava   eesh·too shtaa·va
delicioso.   de·lee·see·o·zoo

The bill, please.
A conta, por favor.   a kong·ta poor
                        fa·*vor*

Shopping

I'd like to buy ...
Queria   ke·*ree*·a
comprar ...   kong·*praar* ...

I'm just looking.
Estou só a ver.   shtoh so a ver

How much is it?
Quanto   kwang·too
custa?   koosh·ta

It's too expensive.
Está muito   shtaa mweeng·too
caro.   kaa·roo

Can you lower the price?
Pode baixar   po·de bai·shaar
o preço?   oo pre·soo

Emergencies
Help!
Socorro!   soo·ko·rroo

Call a doctor!
Chame um   shaa·me oong
médico!   me·dee·koo

Call the police!
Chame a   shaa·me a
polícia!   poo·lee·sya

I'm sick.
Estou doente.   shtoh doo·eng·te

I'm lost.
Estou perdido. (m)   shtoh per·dee·doo
Estou perdida. (f)   shtoh per·dee·da

Where's the toilet?
Onde é a casa de   ong·de e a kaa·za
de banho?   ba·nyoo

Time & Numbers
What time is it?
Que horas são?   kee o·rash sowng

It's (10) o'clock.
São (dez) horas.   sowng (desh) o·rash

Half past (10).
(Dez) e meia.   (desh) e may·a

morning   *manhã*   ma·nyang

afternoon   *tarde*   taar·de

evening   *noite*   noy·te

yesterday	*ontem*	ong·teng
today	*hoje*	o·zhe
tomorrow	*amanhã*	aa·ma·nyang
1	*um*	oong
2	*dois*	doysh
3	*três*	tresh
4	*quatro*	kwaa·troo
5	*cinco*	seeng·koo
6	*seis*	saysh
7	*sete*	se·te
8	*oito*	oy·too
9	*nove*	no·ve
10	*dez*	desh

Transport & Directions
Where's ...?
Onde é ...?   ong·de e ...

What's the address?
Qual é o   kwaal e oo
endereço?   eng·de·re·soo

Can you show me (on the map)?
Pode-me   po·de·me
mostrar   moosh·traar
(no mapa)?   (noo maa·pa)

When's the next bus?
Quando é que sai   kwang·doo e ke sai
o próximo   oo pro·see·moo
autocarro?   ow·to·kaa·rroo

I want to go to ...
Queria ir a ...   ke·ree·a eer a ...

Does it stop at ...?
Pára em ...?   paa·ra eng ...

Please stop here.
Por favor pare   poor fa·vor paa·re
aqui.   a·kee

Index

See also separate subindexes for:

⊗ **Eating p157**

⊕ **Drinking p158**

✪ **Entertainment p158**

🔒 **Shopping p158**

Behind the Scenes

Send Us Your Feedback

We love to hear from travellers – your comments help make our books better. We read every word, and we guarantee that your feedback goes straight to the authors. Visit **lonelyplanet.com/contact** to submit your updates and suggestions.

Note: We may edit, reproduce and incorporate your comments in Lonely Planet products such as guidebooks, websites and digital products, so let us know if you don't want your comments reproduced or your name acknowledged. For a copy of our privacy policy visit lonelyplanet.com/privacy.

Our Readers

Many thanks to the travellers who wrote to us with useful advice and anecdotes: Alexander Baumgärtel, Gill Grinyer, Judith Knott, Liz Graham, Michael Doherty, Robert Bryant, Ronald Pil

Acknowledgements

Cover photograph: Igreja do Carmo, Matt Munro / Lonely Planet ©

Photographs pp28-9 (clockwise from top left): Jeff Greenberg / Getty ©; trabantos / Shutterstock ©; Anastasia Petrova / Shutterstock ©

Kerry's Thanks

I'd like to say a heartfelt *obrigada* to Porto's incredibly welcoming locals, who have helped make this guide what it is. Special thanks go to André Apolinário at Taste Porto for the inside scoop on the city's food scene, Joana Duarte at Visit Porto, and all of the Porto-based guides and port wine pros for their valuable insights.

This Book

This 2nd edition of Lonely Planet's *Pocket Porto* guidebook was researched and written by Kerry Christiani. The previous edition was also written by Kerry. This guidebook was produced by the following:

Destination Editor
Tom Stainer

Senior Product Editor
Genna Patterson

Product Editor
Amanda Williamson

Senior Cartographer
Anthony Phelan

Cartographer
Julie Dodkins

Book Designer
Wibowo Rusli

Assisting Editors Janet Austin, Bruce Evans, Lauren O'Connell

Cover Researcher
Naomi Parker

Thanks to Joel Cotterell, James Hardy, Liz Heynes, Kate Kiely, Anne Mason, Emily McAuliffe, Martine Power

Our Writer

Kerry Christiani

Kerry is an award-winning travel writer, photographer and Lonely Planet author, specialising in central and southern Europe. Based in Wales, she has written for more than a dozen Lonely Planet titles. An adventure addict, she loves mountains, cold places and true wilderness. Her insatiable wanderlust has taken her to all seven continents – from the frozen wilderness of Antarctica to the Australian Outback – and shows no sign of waning. Kerry's writing appears regularly in publications including *Adventure Travel* magazine and she is a *Telegraph* travel expert for Austria and Wales. Kerry features her latest work at https://its-a-small-world.com and tweets @kerrychristiani.

Published by Lonely Planet Global Limited
CRN 554153
2nd edition – Feb 2019
ISBN 978 1 78657 288 2
© Lonely Planet 2019   Photographs © as indicated 2019
10 9 8 7 6 5 4 3 2 1
Printed in Malaysia

Although the authors and Lonely Planet have taken all reasonable care in preparing this book, we make no warranty about the accuracy or completeness of its content and, to the maximum extent permitted, disclaim all liability arising from its use.

All rights reserved. No part of this publication may be copied, stored in a retrieval system, or transmitted in any form by any means, electronic, mechanical, recording or otherwise, except brief extracts for the purpose of review, and no part of this publication may be sold or hired, without the written permission of the publisher. Lonely Planet and the Lonely Planet logo are trademarks of Lonely Planet and are registered in the US Patent and Trademark Office and in other countries. Lonely Planet does not allow its name or logo to be appropriated by commercial establishments, such as retailers, restaurants or hotels. Please let us know of any misuses: lonelyplanet.com/ip.